BE A BETTER STUDENT

Lessons and Worksheets for Teaching Behavior Management in Grades 4–9

Darlene Mannix

Illustrations by Carolyn M. Oesmann

THE CENTER FOR APPLIED RESEARCH IN EDUCATION
West Nyack, New York 10995

ISBN 0-87628-009-2

Library of Congress Cataloging-in-Publication Data

Mannix, Darlene.
    Be a better student : lessons and worksheets for teaching behavior
management in grades 4–9 / Darlene Mannix ; illustrations by Carolyn
M. Oesmann.

        p.   cm.
    ISBN 0-87628-009-2
    1. Classroom management.   2. Behavior modification.   3. School
children—Discipline. I. Title.
LB3013.M327   1989
373.11′024—dc19   89-841
                                                                              CIP

THE CENTER FOR APPLIED
RESEARCH IN EDUCATION
BUSINESS & PROFESSIONAL DIVISION
A division of Simon & Schuster
West Nyack, New York 10995

PRINTED IN THE UNITED STATES OF AMERICA

for Ben

ABOUT THE AUTHOR

Darlene Mannix is a teacher of the emotionally handicapped at South Central Junior-Senior High School in Union Mills, Indiana. She has also taught language disordered, learning disabled, and multiply handicapped students.

Ms. Mannix received her Bachelor of Science degree from Taylor University and her Master's degree in Learning Disabilities from Indiana University. She is a member of the Council for Exceptional Children and has addressed CEC conventions in Virginia and Illinois.

She is the author of *I Can Behave: A Classroom Self-management Curriculum for Elementary Students* (ASIEP Education Company of Portland, Oregon, 1986), *Oral Language Activities for Special Children* (The Center for Applied Research in Education, 1987), and *Sight Word Stories and Seatwork Activities* (Remedia Publications, 1988).

ABOUT THIS BOOK

Be a Better Student is a program for students in grades 4–9 who will profit from specific instruction in behavior management as it relates to school situations. The purpose of the program is to (1) provide students with an overview of basic principles of behavior management, (2) provide examples of school behavior problems and student-models who have used behavior management techniques to attack these problems, (3) provide students with an opportunity to evaluate and discuss the student-model's approach to solving the problem, and (4) provide guidelines for students to use behavior management principles to modify their own behavior or problems at school.

Why is the teaching of behavior management an important task, especially when there are so many demands on a student's school day in terms of academics? Behavior management is usually a course of study that many teachers are required to pursue and then apply to their classes or use with specific students. By the time a student reaches the upper elementary grades, however, several additional considerations make this an even more meaningful skill for the teacher.

First, upper elementary students are beginning to develop higher-level cognitive abilities. They are able to reason (to some degree), understand abstractions, and begin to view situations from alternative perspectives. Why not acknowledge these emerging skills and incorporate them into an overall plan for helping the student to help himself or herself? The student who prides himself or herself on sabotaging the teacher's plans may think twice when given a voice in devising that plan.

Second, many students at this level are exposed to a departmentalized structure in schools, which provides the student with more freedom—often freedom to become lost in the crowd; to wander around a vast, new world without knowing how to adjust and readjust constantly to changing demands of teachers, classes, assignments, and schedules; and to become hopelessly frustrated because his or her disorganization has run rampant. Even the best of caring, interested teachers cannot keep tabs on every book, every assignment, every minute of any student's school life. It is a crucial task for the student to develop coping skills for himself or herself. While students may enjoy the relative freedom given to them, they must keep it under control or risk losing it. The teacher who truly wants to help his or her students must realize that students want and need limits, and that they can learn to structure those limits for themselves.

Finally, consideration must be given to those students who demonstrate noteworthy behavior problems despite having been in an academic environment of school for several years, some no doubt having had individualized instruction and the benefit of special programs. If, after all these teacher-directed attempts have been made, the student is still "lost" without constant teacher guidance or monitoring, perhaps it is time to prioritize behavior management for that student and provide him or her with an in-depth course of study on self-management.

Be a Better Student can be used in a variety of ways with all students. Consider the following factors before implementing the program:

1. *Grouping.* There are several benefits to using the program with an entire class. Students can benefit from other students' ideas and comments about the problems they face in school and ways to solve them. It may be helpful to have the class divided into several small groups when conducting the lesson so that each student benefits from brainstorming and discussing but still is given an opportunity within the small group to share his or her ideas with a few people. Many of the assignments can be done independently after you have taught or clarified the objectives.

2. *Frequency of Use.* If used as a course of study or learning unit, the lessons may be used on a daily basis. About 30–40 minutes per lesson should be sufficient, although you may want to allow additional time for discussion, group problem solving, and the development of individual projects. If behavior change is not a top priority with your students, it can also be used two or three times a week, maintaining continuity of the lessons and frequently reviewing material previously taught. The activities can be graded on a daily basis. Grades can also be given for performance on quizzes, the test following Part One, and their individual projects.

3. *Reading Ability.* The students who use this program do not necessarily have to be good readers to participate in the activities. Although many of the directions suggest calling on volunteers to read the items, a student who can listen well should be able to keep up and understand the principles that are being discussed. Some writing is required to express students' thoughts about situations, plans, and other ideas; however, if used in a small group, the writing itself can be lessened or compensated for by having a student serve as "secretary" for the group. In many cases, you may want to discuss the items orally rather than slow the pace down by having poor readers or writers laboriously fill in blanks.

Be a Better Student is divided into two main sections:

Part One is entitled "All About Behavior." Each of the 20 lessons in this section considers a single aspect of behavior, such as deciding on consequences of a behavior, making the best choice in a situation, setting a goal to modify a behavior, making a plan to realize that goal, evaluating the plan, or rewarding oneself for accomplishments. A problem-solving model is presented with cueing questions for the student to consider when examining a behavior and deciding to modify it. A survey is included near the beginning of this section to allow each student to examine himself or herself and evaluate personal strengths and weaknesses insofar as his or her school setting is concerned. A contract is demonstrated for the student and offers student and teacher an opportunity to make a commitment to learning the material in the program. A test follows this section so that students can receive objective feedback as to their knowledge of this material. The most important consideration for Part One is that the student masters the concepts before going on to the next concept. Many examples are given for each principle, but this is not intended to be an in-depth, comprehensive study. Rather, it is to introduce the student on a very usable, simplistic level to behavior management and what it can do. Students should demonstrate that they have a good grasp of the content in each lesson before moving on to the next lesson. You may want to quiz students on the material and proceed to the next lesson only after all students in the group have demonstrated to your satisfaction that they can meet the objectives specified in each lesson.

Part Two is entitled "Examples of How to Be a Better Student." The 23 lessons provide students with cartoon student-models and three examples of common problem behaviors: turning in assignments on time, doing work carefully, and participating in class. For each example, lessons center on identifying the problem behavior, devising a plan, providing the student with exercises in evaluating the student-model as he or she tries out the plan, record keeping, and finally evaluating the plan and suggesting modifications. Then, the student is given an opportunity to carry the behavior change program one step farther by implementing the techniques demonstrated by the student-model in the student's own school situation. The student sets up his or her own plan for changing behavior and tries it out for a predetermined length of time—usually one or two weeks. After this systematic field practice, the student goes through the evaluation process on his or her own plan and determines whether or not it has helped him or her to "be a better student." Care must be given in Part Two to ensure that the students do not get "bogged down" in working through the problems of the student-model. Although a plan and goal are suggested for each student-model, situations may differ from conditions in your own school. Even if the situations are different, it would help the student to complete the exercises given for the student-model to ensure that he or she is adequately perceiving the situations presented and keeping track of the behavior he or she is supposed to monitor correctly. Later, when the student is requested to carry out his or her own plan and program, it may be more practical to adapt some of the ideas to fit your own situation.

The student-models in *Be a Better Student* represent only a sampling of the behaviors that are necessary for top-notch student performance. You may want to focus on only one aspect of a behavior rather than try to improve several related behaviors at the same time, as the student-models do. The appendix provides a breakdown of related problems that may be helped by techniques or forms that have been presented in the behavior change plans of the student-models in the book. The problem behavior is specified, a specific skill to be learned is identified, and a helpful form or technique is listed. All forms may be modified, if necessary, to meet the specific needs of each class and student.

Use these lessons as they are; then expand upon them as you desire. You'll see the results when your students are able to modify and manage their behavior successfully. Best wishes to you and your students!

Darlene Mannix

CONTENTS

Part Two
Examples of How to Be a Better Student

Appendix
Skills Index and Additional Forms

BE A BETTER STUDENT

Part One

ALL ABOUT BEHAVIOR

Lesson 1   LET ME OUT OF HERE!

Overview

This lesson introduces the philosophy behind this book, namely, that one can choose intelligently to make his or her school existence tolerable (if not actually pleasurable) by exercising control over those variables that can be controlled. This lesson draws parallels between school and prison in the sense that both require adherence to rules and staying "within the system" in order to come out ahead (or, in prison, to come out at all!). The point stressed is that students have choices that can affect their freedom. They can choose to be nonconformists in ways that will ultimately deprive them of the very freedoms that they truly desire (for example, the greatest football player on the team can't show off his athletic ability if he received two F's on his report card and is off the team). Or students can enjoy an expanded repertoire of privileges by making intelligent choices that reflect working "within the system," such as passing Biology 101 the first time around and then getting the privilege of taking Computer Lab or working in the audiovisual room instead of repeating Biology 101.

Lesson Objective

- Students will be able to state at least one reason why it is advantageous to get along well at school.

Teacher Preparation

1. Make enough copies of Worksheet 1-1, "Let Me Out of Here!," for your students.
2. Copy the following on the chalkboard:

School (is like) prison because both are	Getting along well at school is important because
1.	1.
2.	2.
3.	3.

Lesson Plan

1. Introduce the lesson by stating that the students will be doing some thinking about freedom and making choices to keep their freedoms. You may want to use some of the following questions:

   a. What does it mean to be free or have freedom?

   b. Does freedom mean you can do anything you want to do?

   c. Does it mean you can do anything you want to as long as it doesn't hurt anyone else or get you in trouble?

2. Conclude the discussion by stating that they are going to be thinking about how they can have personal freedom at school.

3. Distribute Worksheet 1-1.

4. Direct the students' attention to the cartoons at the top. Ask, "How is school like a prison?" Record students' answers on the chalkboard. You may have more than three answers and want to keep a longer list.

   Suggestions might include having to "play the game" in school and stay out of trouble, "serving their time," resisting the limitations on their personal freedom, being somewhere where they would rather not be, eating institutionalized food, and wearing clothing that is approved by authority.

5. Discuss the questions on the worksheet. You may want to call on individual students to read the question and respond. Or you might have students write out their answers on the worksheet first and then discuss them as a group later. Answers may include

---

1. Opinion.
2. Opinion.
3. Good behavior may lead to a reduced sentence, and vice versa.
4. Good school behavior may keep you out of trouble, so teachers will trust you more and allow you to have more freedom.
5. More fun to do what you want than follow rules, hang around with kids who want to get in trouble, not really understand the rules or think the rules make sense.
6. You'll stay out of trouble, people won't hassle you, you might learn something.
7. Opinion.
8. Opinion.

---

6. Ask students to think about how getting along well at school might give them more freedom. Record students' answers on the chalkboard.

7. ASSIGNMENT: Inform students that in the next lesson, the first thing you are going to ask them is to state at least one reason why it is to their advantage to get along well at school.

8. Tell students to file their worksheet in their folders.

LET ME OUT OF HERE!

Questions

1. Do you ever feel that school is like a prison? _____

2. Why? _____
_____

3. What are some ways that behavior affects freedom in prison? _____
_____

4. What are some ways that behavior affects freedom in school? _____
_____

5. Why do you think that staying out of trouble is hard for some kids? _____

6. What are some advantages of getting along with the system at school? _____

7. What might you have to give up to get along well at school? _____
_____

8. What might you gain by getting along well at school? _____
_____

Lesson 2   TWO KINDS OF STUDENTS

Overview

This lesson presents the idea that student "types" can fit into one of two categories: *good* or *could be better*. The idea of having the categories "good" and "bad" is discarded because a "bad" student can be thought of as one who just hasn't developed some skills in making good choices. The potential is still there! Students may tend to classify themselves as "bad" students, but after examining their reasons, it should be evident that they have "bad" habits or have made poor choices for themselves as far as getting along at school is concerned.

Lesson Objectives

- Students will be able to state at least three characteristics of a "good" student.
- Students will be able to state at least three characteristics of a "could be better" student.

Teacher Preparation

1. Make enough copies of Worksheet 2-1, "Two Kinds of Students," for your students.
2. Copy the following on the chalkboard:

> Good Student   Bad Student

Lesson Plan

1. Remind students that in the previous lesson, they discussed how being in school might put some limits on them, but it also might allow them to experience making choices that would give them freedoms.

   Ask students to write (or be prepared to answer orally) at least one reason why it is important for them to get along well at school. You can collect their responses for a grade or simply discuss their answers as a group.

6

2. Introduce Lesson 2 by stating that students can be divided into two groups. Ask for suggestions as to how students could be grouped, such as girls/boys, good/bad/, freshmen/sophomores, junior high/senior high.

3. Call attention to the "Good" and "Bad" written on the board. Ask students to suggest some characteristics of a "good" student, and write them on the board. Suggestions are "always does homework," "is polite to the teacher," "never loses his or her pencil." Then ask students to suggest some characteristics of a "bad" student, such as "skips class," "is loud," "doesn't do his or her homework," and write these on the chalkboard.

4. Distribute Worksheet 2-1.

5. Direct students' attention to the cartoon at the top. Ask and discuss, "Is it really easy to tell 'good' students from 'bad' students as the picture shows?" "Are kids really either 'good' or 'bad' students?"

6. Inform the students that they are going to think about the characteristics on the worksheet and decide whether or not that would describe the first kid ("good") or the second (they will want to label him "bad," but tell them to hold off on the label for a minute or two).

7. Discuss the responses to the worksheet. Ask students why the comment described Student A or B. Here are the answers:

```
1. Student B
2. Student A
3. Student A
4. Student B
5. Student B
6. Student A
7. Student B
8. Student B
9. Student A
10. Student B
```

8. Ask students to examine closely the characteristics that describe Student B. Have students decide whether or not the characteristic means Student B is a *bad person* or made a *bad choice*. Have students suggest a better choice for each situation. Here are suggested responses:

1. BAD CHOICE—Student B should fly his airplane outside or after school.

4. BAD HABIT—Student B should learn to keep track of his materials.

5. BAD CHOICE—Student B should organize his time or priorities better.

7. BAD CHOICE—Student B should consider the consequences of getting an F.

8. BAD CHOICE—Student B should have obeyed the law about pulling a fire alarm.

10. BAD HABIT—Student B should do his sleeping at home.

9. Cross out the word "Bad" on the board and suggest the term "Could Be Better" to students. Look over the characteristics that are listed on the board under this column. Have students suggest ways that these characteristics could be improved.

10. Explain that even "Good" students could improve certain aspects of themselves, but that for purposes of this book, the terms "Good" and "Could Be Better" will be used to describe those students who have fairly good school skills and can make good school choices as opposed to those students who need to develop some skills to make better choices and be better students.

11. REVIEW: Ask students to identify three characteristics of a "good" student. Ask students to identify three characteristics of a "could be better" student.

12. ASSIGNMENT: Inform students that in the next lesson, the first thing they will do is state three characteristics of "good" and "could be better" students. Their assignment is to review the material on the board. (Students may want to copy some of the comments on the board.)

13. Tell students to file their worksheet in their folders.

Name _____ Date _____

TWO KINDS OF STUDENTS

Does this comment describe Student A or Student B?

_____ 1. "I can't wait to fly this airplane in study hall."

_____ 2. "I must remember to read over my science notes for the test tomorrow."

_____ 3. "I just love algebra!"

_____ 4. "Where did that pencil go?"

_____ 5. "I don't have time to do that assignment—I've got a party to go to."

_____ 6. "I'll ask Mr. Wise if I can help him make his bulletin board."

_____ 7. "I don't care if I get an 'F'—doesn't that stand for 'Fantastic'?"

_____ 8. "Suspension? You must be joking! Just because I pulled the fire alarm? It was just a joke."

_____ 9. "I need all these books for my class."

_____ 10. "I'm so glad I have English next hour—that's my favorite class to sleep through."

Lesson 3   WHAT KIND OF STUDENT ARE YOU?

Overview

Now that students have some familiarity with characteristics of "good" and "could be better" student classifications, an attempt is made to personalize these characteristics for the student. They are asked to think about their own habits or tendencies and decide how they would rate themselves. At the conclusion of the lesson, the student is asked to decide if he or she could be a better student and to list a few areas in which he or she could improve. The student is also asked to list some areas of strength. This lesson is setting the student up eventually to choose an area to work on to improve specific behaviors at school.

Lesson Objectives

- Students will identify themselves as a "could be better" student.
- Students will identify at least one area or behavior that they could improve in at school.

Teacher Preparation

Make enough copies of Worksheet 3-1, "What Kind of Student Are You?" and Worksheet 3-2, "Student Behavior Survey," for your students.

Lesson Plan

1. Remind students that in the previous lesson, they discussed characteristics of "good" and "could be better" students. At this time, have them list (or state orally, if you prefer) three characteristics of each type. Discuss or collect and grade their responses.
2. Introduce today's lesson by stating that they are going to evaluate themselves as students and think about areas in which they are already "good" students and areas in which they could improve.
3. Distribute Worksheet 3-1.
4. Direct students' attention to the cartoon at the top. Remind them that you can't always tell just by looking if someone is a good or could be better student; it's more by what someone *does*.
5. Have students complete the worksheet by circling YES or NO to each of the comments listed.
6. Discuss the comments. Questions may include

1. Why would having a sharpened pencil make people think you were a good student?
2. Why is paying attention a good habit for good students?
3. Why is writing down assignments something that would help someone be a better student?
4. If someone forgets his or her homework once, does that mean he or she is not a good student?
5. Why is it important to ask the teacher for help when you don't understand something?
6. Why is it important to turn in assignments on the due date? If you turn them in eventually, isn't that okay?
7. Why is waiting your turn for help important?
8. What are some ways that students disturb other students in a classroom?
9. What difference does studying before a test make?
10. If your answers are correct, why should it matter if your paper is neat or not?

7. Have students evaluate themselves by filling out the blanks at the bottom of the worksheet. Probably some students will insist that they are *good* students, having no faults whatever. Rather than contradict them at this time, accept their response but indicate that just about everyone can find room to improve in at least one area. Ask them to be very conscious the next few days of the things that teachers tell them to do, as this might give them some clues on areas that they could improve in.

8. REVIEW: Ask students to identify the two groups of students. Ask students to state two characteristics of each group. Ask students to specify which of the two groups is more characteristic of themselves. Ask students to identify at least one behavior that is a problem or area for improvement for them.

9. ASSIGNMENT: Distribute Worksheet 3-2 to the students. Read the directions to them and explain that they are going to compare the answers they put down now with the answers they will write down at the end of this course. It is hoped that there will be a change! Inform them that the assignment is due at the beginning of class tomorrow.

10. Tell students to file Worksheet 3-1 in their folder and to keep Worksheet 3-2 in a conspicuous place until it is finished.

Name _____ Date _____

WHAT KIND OF STUDENT ARE YOU?

Does this comment describe you? Circle YES or NO.

1.	"I always have a sharpened pencil and lots of paper."	YES	NO
2.	"I pay attention while the teacher is talking."	YES	NO
3.	"I write down my assignments so I won't forget."	YES	NO
4.	"I always do my homework."	YES	NO
5.	"I ask the teacher when I don't understand something."	YES	NO
6.	"I turn in my assignments when they are due."	YES	NO
7.	"I wait my turn when I need to ask the teacher about something."	YES	NO
8.	"I don't disturb other students in the room."	YES	NO
9.	"I spend time studying material before class or a test."	YES	NO
10.	"My papers are neat and well organized."	YES	NO

Are you a GOOD student? _____

Could you be a BETTER student? _____

Name ——————————————————— Date ———————————————————

STUDENT BEHAVIOR SURVEY

Please complete this survey honestly. Save this survey to compare your answers with those of the survey at the end of the course.

1. Do you think you are a good student now? ———————————————

2. Do you think you could be a better student? ———————————————

3. What are some things that you are good at in school?

   a. ————————————————————————————————————

   b. ————————————————————————————————————

   c. ————————————————————————————————————

4. What are some things that people would say about you that make you sound like a good student?

   a. ————————————————————————————————————

   b. ————————————————————————————————————

   c. ————————————————————————————————————

5. What are some things that are hard for you at school?

   a. ————————————————————————————————————

   b. ————————————————————————————————————

   c. ————————————————————————————————————

6. What are some things that you do that do not make people think you are a good student?

   a. ————————————————————————————————————

   b. ————————————————————————————————————

   c. ————————————————————————————————————

7. What is the one main thing you would like to improve about yourself at school?

   ————————————————————————————————————

   ————————————————————————————————————

Lesson 4 "A" FOR EFFORT

Overview

Once the student has identified an area that he or she acknowledges as one that could be improved, the next step is for the student to make a commitment toward improving that behavior. This commitment is demonstrated by the *effort* that the student puts forth toward changing or improving that problem area. The student must take ownership of the problem; he or she must realize that it will take dedication on *his* or *her* part to see some progress. The purpose of this lesson is to indicate to the student that effort is going to play a major role in successfully improving his or her behavior, not the efforts of others, but of himself or herself.

Lesson Objectives

- Students will identify themselves as being the primary person responsible for making themselves better students.
- Students will identify the quality of *effort* as being one of the most important factors in making their plan succeed.

Teacher Preparation

1. Make enough copies of Worksheet 4-1, "'A' for Effort," for your students.
2. Copy the following on the chalkboard:

$$\boxed{\text{E}}$$

Lesson Plan

1. Remind students that in the previous lesson, they talked about what kind of student they were. Review briefly some characteristics of "good" and "could be better" students. Ask students to have Worksheet 3-2, "Student Behavior Survey," handy and be ready to discuss their responses.
2. Briefly check to make sure that students have completed the survey sheet. Ask students to share responses on a volunteer basis, as some may view this as a personal matter and not want to have their answers revealed to the class. You may want to commend students for having their assignment done and award a grade or extra points for this.

14

3. Have students file Worksheet 3-2 in their folders.

4. Introduce today's lesson by stating that they are going to discover who the single most important person is in making changes in themselves. They are also going to learn about an important ingredient that is essential to making changes in their behavior.

5. Direct the students' attention to the "E" on the chalkboard. Explain that this important ingredient starts with this letter. Ask them to be thinking about what word could describe that ingredient.

6. Distribute Worksheet 4-1.

7. Direct students' attention to the first cartoon. Ask for a volunteer to read the question and give an answer. Discuss

    a. How does the cartoon show ways that parents and/or teachers try to get students to be better students?

    b. Do you think those methods work?

    c. What if the student is only working for a reward?

8. Direct students' attention to the middle cartoon. Ask for a volunteer to read the question and give an answer. Discuss

    a. Why didn't this student's plan of studying work?

    b. Do you think he should try studying more than just once?

    c. Why didn't studying help him?

9. Direct students' attention to the bottom cartoon. Ask for a volunteer to read the question and give an answer. Discuss

    a. What are three different plans that these three students came up with for being better students?

    b. Is there only one right way to be a better student?

    c. Can you think of a word that starts with "E" that could describe the ingredient to being a better student?

10. REVIEW: Ask students to identify the most important person responsible for making themselves better students. Ask students to state one very important ingredient that is important to making their plans to be better students succeed.

11. ASSIGNMENT: Tell students that in tomorrow's lesson, they will have a short quiz that covers the material in the first four lessons. To study for this quiz, they should review their worksheets from the first four lessons. They should know

    a. At least one reason why it is important to get along at school.

    b. Three characteristics of "good" and "could be better" students.

    c.   At least one area in which they could improve in school .

    d.   The person who is most responsible for making them become better students.

    e.   One important ingredient that will make their plans to become better students succeed.

12. Tell students to file Worksheet 4-1 in their folders.

"A" FOR EFFORT

1. *Who* needs to want to become a better student?

2. *Who* needs to work hard at becoming a better student?

3. *Who* needs to work out a plan to become a better student?

Lesson 5   REVIEW LESSON

Overview

In most academic classes, students are frequently given quizzes that cover material discussed in class. These lessons, similarly, have concepts and facts that the student will need to know—and know *well*. To introduce the concept of "mastery learning" to the student, quizzes will frequently appear that *must* be passed before the class can proceed to the next lessons. Point out to the students that in every lesson, they have been given an objective that tells them what they are responsible for knowing and a review session in which they have heard the highlights of the lesson again. If they have been keeping up with the material by completing assignments and reviewing daily, they should have no problem whatever in getting a perfect score on the quiz. It is important that the students come to view these quizzes as an opportunity to *shine*, to show how much they have learned (to convince *themselves* as much as their teacher!).

Lesson Objective

- Students will demonstrate mastery of material covered in the first four lessons by scoring 90% or above on the quiz.

Teacher Preparation

Make enough copies of Worksheet 5-1, "Quiz," for your students.

Lesson Plan

1. Remind students that they will be taking a quiz that covers material discussed in the first four lessons. Ask if there are any last-minute questions.
2. Distribute Worksheet 5-1.
3. Allow time for students to complete the quiz.
4. Scoring:

> 1. Answers will vary. (1 point)
> 2. Answers will vary. (3 points)
> 3. Answers will vary. (3 points)
> 4. Answers will vary. (1 point)
> 5. Me, myself, I am.   (1 point)
> 6. Effort.   (1 point)

5. Discuss answers and make corrections if necessary.

6. Tell students to file the quiz in their folders.

7. ASSIGNMENT: Students who scored 90% or above have no specific assignment for the next lesson. Students who scored below 90% should copy the question(s) missed and the correct answer(s). This is to be handed in before the next class time.

QUIZ

Briefly answer each question below.

1. Give one reason why it is important to get along at school:

   _____

   _____

2. List three characteristics of "good" students:

   a. _____

   b. _____

   c. _____

3. List three characteristics of "could be better" students:

   a. _____

   b. _____

   c. _____

4. What is one area in which *you* could improve in school?

   _____

   _____

5. Who is the person most responsible for helping someone become a better student?

   _____

6. What is one important ingredient that will help you become a better student?

   _____

Total points possible: 10   My score: _____

Lesson 6 LET'S MAKE A DEAL

Overview

Contracting is one technique that has been useful in maintaining or increasing behaviors that are desirable in students. It is a straightforward, unemotional, binding, fair document that spells out plainly what both parties are expected to do. This technique is very helpful when dealing with students who tend to misquote the teacher ("You never said that!" "You said we didn't have to do that." "You told me I could have . . ."), students who do not wish to share the responsibility for their learning ("What kind of teacher are you? Giving me a D-!"), or students who need to know that some sort of reward is coming for their effort (even if the reward is just the end of the lessons). While going over the contract with the students, be sure to note the following points:

1. The student should read and indicate that he or she understands the behaviors expected of him or her. In this contract, the student's responsibilities are reading and studying the lessons in this book and taking a test at the end of Part One.

2. The teacher also has responsibilities for keeping the contract. He or she is to assist the student in understanding the material, praise the student, and administer the reward at the end.

3. The student and teacher should agree on an appropriate reward for completion of the material and performance of the test. Rewards may include prizes supplied by the teacher, activity reinforcers (free time), special privileges (movie, skipping homework), or other rewards that the teacher and student have agreed on as being appropriate.

4. The *bonus* reward is reserved for students who have performed particularly well on the test. The score (%) that must be achieved on the test should also be agreed upon at this time.

5. The expiration date of the contract serves to give the students a timetable or framework within which he or she has to complete assignments. The date should be reasonable and should take into account the amount of time that the class will be spending on the workbook as well as the ability of the students to absorb the material. It is hoped that the contract would not have to extend more than one grading period (or four to six weeks).

6. Signatures of the student, teacher, and a witness are required at the bottom of the contract, as well as the date of the signing and initiation of the contract. These features add legitimacy to the contract.

For referral, the student may want to have a copy of this document in his or her behavior file. You may want to display all the contracts in a prominent place in the room as a visual reminder of the importance of living up to the demands of the contract—for both parties.

Lesson Objectives

- Students will demonstrate knowledge of the behavior contract by stating the student's responsibilities, teacher's responsibilities, reward, and date of expiration of the contract.
- Students will, in good faith, sign the behavior contract.

Teacher Preparation

1. Make enough copies of Worksheet 6-1, "Official Contract," for your students.
2. Copy the following on the chalkboard:

Student	Teacher	Rewards

Lesson Plan

1. Introduce this lesson by asking students what they know about contracts. You might explain that when you buy something, such as a car, you might have to sign a contract promising that you will pay for it. Similarly, you might sign a contract if you join a health club, promising that you will make your payments. Students might have other experiences with contracts (for example, a movie contract, contracts for a job, providing services for others).
2. Explain that they will be given a contract to read over and consider that goes along with the next few lessons. Both the student and the teacher have commitments to making the contract work, and each needs to understand what the other's jobs are.
3. Distribute Worksheet 6-1.
4. Direct students' attention to the first paragraph. Ask them to read it over silently or have a volunteer read it aloud for the class.
5. Under "Student" on the chalkboard, summarize the main responsibilities of the student in this contract:

```
Student
1. Learn about behavior.
2. Take a test.
```

6. Direct students' attention to the second paragraph. Again, read silently or have a student volunteer read it aloud.

7. Under "Teacher" on the chalkboard, summarize the main responsibilities of the teacher in this contract:

```
Teacher
1. Help with problems.
2. Praise the student.
3. Provide reward.
```

8. Explain to the students that after taking the test at the end of Lesson 20, they will be eligible for a reward. Rewards will be discussed in greater depth in a later lesson, but it will be sufficient at this point to have students select one of the following types of rewards:

- school materials (folder, pen, school button)
- free class period to listen to music
- a movie in class
- a night without homework

You may solicit student input for rewards that they would be interested in earning and list them under "Rewards" on the board.

9. Have students fill in their names on the top line of the contract.

10. Have students fill in the teacher's name in the second paragraph.

11. Have students select a reward from those listed (and approved by the teacher) on the board and write it on the line in the third paragraph.

12. Explain that the *bonus* reward is given only to those students who score exceptionally high on the test. You may specify 90% as the cutoff, for example. Any student scoring that high would automatically receive the bonus reward, which should be decided upon at this time. It should be

something that is more desirable than the "ordinary" rewards for just completing the lessons. Examples include

- a class party for those students
- a special field trip
- passes to a movie
- coupons for hamburgers
- swimming (if you have access to a pool)

Have students select and fill in the name of their chosen bonus reward.

13. Decide on an expiration date. Consider how many lessons you will need to cover, how many times a week you will be working on the lessons, how many vacations, snow days, and other interruptions may be likely to occur, and come up with an approximate timetable for when the lessons will be completed.

14. Have students sign and date the contract. Circulate around the room and sign each completed contract. Allow students to choose a witness to view this procedure.

15. Tell students to file the contract in their folders. As mentioned, you may want to display copies of the contract around the room to remind all parties of their obligations.

Name _____ Date _____

OFFICIAL CONTRACT

I, _____, realize that there are many things I can do to
　　　　　(your name)
become a better student. I also realize that the most important thing I can do to help myself is to

TRY. To become a better student, I will

1. Try to learn about behavior and how I can change my behavior by reading and studying the lessons in this book.
2. Take a test at the end of Part One to see how much I have learned about behavior.

My teacher, _____, also realizes that becoming a better
　　　　　　　　　(teacher's name)
student is hard work and will require some work on his or her part to help me. Therefore, he or she

will

1. Assist me with any problems I have understanding the lessons in this part of the book at a mutually convenient time.
2. Praise and encourage me for making the effort to do a good job on the lessons.
3. Make sure that I get the reward I have chosen after taking the test at the end of Part One, depending on my score.

After studying the lessons and taking the test, I will receive the reward I have chosen below:

_____

If my score on the test is _____ %, I will also receive the BONUS reward of:

_____

This contract expires _____
　　　　　　　　　　　　　　　　　　　(date)

Student's signature _____   Teacher's signature _____

Today's date _____   Witness _____

Lesson 7   WHAT IS A BEHAVIOR?

Overview

In this lesson, the students are introduced to the concept of behavior, simply defined as something that you *do*. If students are familiar with *verbs,* you may want to assist them in their thinking by calling attention to words that end in *-ing*. At the beginning of each lesson (from Lesson 7 through Lesson 18) is a section labeled "Know This." The idea, fact, or term that you want the student to learn is highlighted here, as well as at the end of the lesson in the review. For ease in visually coding or writing the terms, the symbol Ⓑis introduced, and is used throughout the lessons to cue the student to think about *behavior.*

Lesson Objectives

- Students will identify five behaviors that would be likely to occur at school.
- Students will correctly identify from a list of items those items that are behaviors.
- Students will identify the symbol Ⓑ as *behavior.*

Teacher Preparation

1. Make enough copies of Worksheet 7-1, "What Is a Behavior?," for your students.
2. Copy the following on the chalkboard:

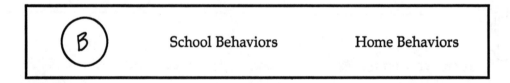

Lesson Plan

1. Introduce this lesson by telling the students that they will be learning about behaviors, that you will define for them as something that they can do.
2. Point to the Ⓑsymbol on the board. Inform students that in this and later lessons when you are discussing *behaviors,* you will use this symbol as a quick way of writing "behavior" or "behaviors."

3. Distribute Worksheet 7-1.

4. Direct students' attention to the "Know This" box. Inform them that definitions for the terms or concepts they will need to know for each lesson will be found at the beginning of the worksheets. They will be expected to know that information.

5. Call on a student volunteer to read the definition.

6. Ask for examples of items that would be considered behaviors. Include any identifiable action verb (running, playing, yelling) and words that indicate mental activity (thinking, praying). To simplify matters, it is easier to categorize a behavior as something that can be observed and a nonbehavior as something that happens that a person doesn't really cause to happen. For that reason, most of the nonbehaviors are considered as acts of nature that end in *-ing*. In later lessons, students will be asked to identify behaviors that they would like to change. By gearing their thinking toward observable actions they can control, you will simplify the later tasks greatly.

7. Under the "Examples" section of the worksheet, have students list three behaviors and three nonbehaviors.

8. Direct students' attention to the board. Ask students to list several behaviors that would most likely occur at school (such as cleaning out a locker, going to a school dance, cleaning off a cafeteria tray) and several behaviors that would most likely occur at home (such as watching television, reading the newspaper, washing the car).

9. Under the "Try This" section of the worksheet, have students complete the activity independently. Check responses as a group and discuss any questions. Here are the answers:

Behaviors are 1, 2, 4, 5, 8, 9, 10.

10. Direct students' attention to the "Review" box on the worksheet. Have students complete the missing word. (do)

11. REVIEW: Ask students to identify five behaviors that would be likely to occur at school. Ask students to define *behavior.*

12. ASSIGNMENT: Inform students that they will be asked to give examples of some school behaviors tomorrow and will be asked to define behavior. Ask for them to look for some unusual examples throughout the day.

13. Tell students to file Worksheet 7-1 in their folders.

WHAT IS A BEHAVIOR?

Know This: A behavior is something that you do—you make it happen.

Examples: Ⓑ   Ⓑ̸

1. _____   1. _____

2. _____   2. _____

3. _____   3. _____

Try This: Which of the following items are behaviors? Put a Ⓑ in front of each behavior. (*Think:* Is it something I can do?)

_____ 1. opening a locker

_____ 2. dancing in the gym

_____ 3. the wind blowing through the trees

_____ 4. throwing a football

_____ 5. smiling

_____ 6. leaves falling

_____ 7. ice melting

_____ 8. doing biology homework

_____ 9. thinking about a friend

_____ 10. laughing at a joke

Review: A behavior is something you _____.

Lesson 8   IT USUALLY HAPPENS HERE

Overview

This lesson starts the students thinking about the setting in which certain behaviors are most likely to occur. At this point, the student is not asked to consider the *appropriateness* of the behavior in that setting, but merely the likelihood of it occurring. As the student progresses through these lessons, he or she will be identifying behaviors that he or she would like to improve. One consideration the student will face is that of ensuring that the environment will be more conducive to that behavior occurring. For example, if a student wants to study more effectively, he would probably experience more success if his studying took place in a library than on the 50-yard line at a football game. If a student wanted to make friends with other students, she will probably need to be in a setting where there are people, such as the school cafeteria rather than a deserted alley.

Lesson Objective

- Students will identify places at which certain behaviors would most likely be observed.

Teacher Preparation

1. Make enough copies of Worksheet 8-1, "It Usually Happens Here," for the students.
2. Copy the following on the chalkboard:

Restaurant	Bowling Alley
1.	1.
2.	2.

Lesson Plan

1. Review yesterday's material by asking students to give some examples of school behaviors that they observed during the day. Ask students to define what a behavior is (something that you do).

2. Introduce today's lesson by stating that some behaviors are more likely to occur in certain places. This is important to know because later, when they are working on changing their behavior, they will want to pick good places to work on this, places that lend themselves to having these behaviors happen.

3. Direct the students' attention to the chalkboard. Tell the students that you want them to think about and list several behaviors that would be likely to happen at each of those places. Ask students for ideas and list them on the board. Answers may include

---

Restaurant

1. Talk to a waitress.
2. Be served a glass of water.
3. Leave a tip.
4. Look at a menu.

Bowling Alley

1. Wear bowling shoes.
2. Throw a bowling ball.
3. Keep score.
4. Cheer loudly.

---

4. Distribute Worksheet 8-1.

5. Direct students' attention to the "Know This" box. Inform them that they will need to know and understand this point. Call on a student volunteer to read the sentence.

6. Direct students' attention to the "Examples" section. Have the students discuss and complete this section with examples of behaviors that would probably occur in each of those four settings. Answers might include

---

Home

1. Wash dishes.
2. Sleep.

Movie

1. Eat popcorn.
2. Stand in line.

School

1. Clean out a locker.
2. Take a test.

Hospital

1. Get a shot.
2. Have surgery.

---

7. Direct students' attention to the "Try This" section. Call on a student volunteer to read the directions. Have students complete the activity independently and discuss their responses as a group.

8. Have students complete the missing words from the "Review" section at the bottom of the worksheet. Answers are

    A behavior is something that you (do).

    Some behaviors usually happen at certain (places).

9. ASSIGNMENT: Inform students that tomorrow you will ask them to identify several behaviors that would most likely occur at certain places. Ask them to think of some unusual places that would lend themselves to having certain behaviors happen there.

10. Tell students to file Worksheet 8-1 in their folders.

IT USUALLY HAPPENS HERE

> *Know This:* Some behaviors usually happen at certain places.

Examples:

Home	School	Movie	Hospital
1._____	1._____	1._____	1._____
2._____	2._____	2._____	2._____

Try This: Where would you most likely see or do these behaviors? There may be more than one correct answer!

1. Study for a test _____

2. Wash your hair _____

3. Play racquetball _____

4. Laugh with friends _____

5. Cry _____

6. Type a paper _____

7. Deposit a check _____

8. Clean out your locker _____

9. Sharpen a pencil _____

10. Argue with a teacher _____

Review:

A behavior is something that you _____.

Some behaviors usually happen at certain _____.

Lesson 9   ARE THESE THE BEST CONDITIONS?

Overview

This lesson carries the idea of behavior occurring at certain places a bit farther by introducing the idea of appropriateness. Some behaviors, in and of themselves, are neutral until placed in context. For example, is "playing" an appropriate or inappropriate behavior? One wouldn't be able to answer that question unless a context were provided. "Playing" might be appropriate on a baseball field, but not in the middle of math class. The student in this lesson is asked to evaluate the appropriateness of behaviors given a particular situation.

Lesson Objectives

- Students will identify the most appropriate conditions for a given behavior to occur, given a choice of several situations.
- Students will state why a given behavior may cause or be a problem if it occurred in a situation that is not appropriate.

Teacher Preparation

1. Make enough copies of Worksheet 9-1, "Are These the Best Conditions?," for your students.
2. Copy the following on the chalkboard:

> Best Conditions—Time and Place

Lesson Plan

1. Review yesterday's material by asking students what "It usually happens here" means. (where a behavior is likely to occur)
2. Continue the review by informing students that you will name a place and would like them to supply at least two behaviors that would probably occur at that place, for example,

   - hospital—get stitches, have an operation
   - day care center—children coloring, children swinging

- math class—students adding, students using a calculator
- P.E. class—students bowling, students playing field hockey

3. Continue the review by asking students for their ideas of unusual places and behaviors that would most likely occur there.

4. Introduce today's lesson by stating that today they are going to be concentrating on the appropriateness of a behavior happening at a certain time or place. Refer to the chalkboard.

5. Ask students to identify several behaviors that would be appropriate for P.E. class but not for a geometry class. (Ideas may include talking without raising hand, getting out of one's seat, having equipment to be thrown around, and so on.)

6. Distribute Worksheet 9-1.

7. Direct students' attention to the "Know This" box. Inform students that for a behavior to be appropriate, it should occur at the right or best time and place.

8. Direct students' attention to the "Try This" section. Call on student volunteers to read the directions, examples, and two conditions for each example. Discuss responses. Answers are

> 1. first column
> 2. second column
> 3. second column
> 4. first column
> 5. second column
> 6. second column

9. Have students complete the missing words from the "Review" section at the bottom of the worksheet.

> A behavior is something that you (do).
>
> Some behaviors usually occur or happen at certain (places).
>
> Sometimes there is a (better) time or place for a behavior to happen.

10. ASSIGNMENT: Ask students to choose one of their classes to use for this assignment. During that class, they are to list three appropriate behaviors that occurred during class time and three inappropriate behaviors that occurred. Students may want to make a chart to record their observations. These observations will be discussed as part of tomorrow's lesson.

11. Tell students to file Worksheet 9-1 in their folders.

ARE THESE THE BEST CONDITIONS?

Know This: Sometimes there is a *better* time or place for a behavior to occur.

Try This: Think about each behavior below. Circle the answer that describes the best conditions for each behavior to occur. Why might it cause a problem if the behavior occurred under the other conditions?

	At This Time and Place?	*Or This?*
1. Doing homework	during study hall	during a football game
2. Opening a locker	in the middle of class	between classes
3. Cleaning out your desk	while the teacher is giving an assignment	after the teacher has given the assignment
4. Asking the teacher what your homework was	before class	while the teacher is talking to the principal
5. Sleeping	during math class	after school
6. Throwing a ball	before math class starts	during P.E.

Review:
A behavior is something that you

_____.

Some behaviors usually occur at

certain _____.

Sometimes there is a _____

_____ time or place for

a behavior to happen.

Lesson 10   THE CHOICE IS YOURS

Overview

In this lesson, students are introduced to the idea that in most situations they encounter, there are several behavior choices for them. Without consciously thinking about it, they weigh the alternatives and choose to behave in a certain way. (In later lessons, the idea of choosing in order to get closer to a goal is discussed.) The purpose of this lesson is to give the student practice in thinking of alternative behaviors for a given situation and deciding which is the best choice.

Lesson Objectives

- Given a situation, students will generate at least three behavior options for that situation.
- Students will state at least one reason why the selected behavior for a given situation is most appropriate for those conditions.

Teacher Preparation

1. Make enough copies of Worksheet 10-1, "The Choice Is Yours," for your students.
2. Copy the following on the chalkboard:

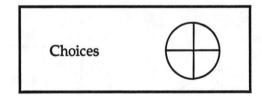

Lesson Plan

1. Briefly review yesterday's lesson by asking students to give a summary of the lesson, for example, deciding on the appropriateness of a behavior at a time or place.
2. Discuss the assignment from yesterday by having students volunteer information about their findings from observing appropriate and inappropriate behavior in their selected class.
3. Introduce today's lesson by stating that in most situations, there are several options that a person has as far as choosing what behavior is

going to occur. Ask students to supply at least three different behaviors that could occur in the following situations:

a. Your uncle gave you $50 to spend anyway you want (buy records, buy a lot of junk food, save it, give some to a friend).

b. Your father said you had to finish taking out all 20 bags of trash before you could go to the movies with your friends (take out the garbage right away, try to sneak out, get your brother to help, try bargaining with your father).

4. Direct students' attention to the board. Explain that the symbol on the board is going to stand for the different choices of behavior that we have in situations. You might ask students if they have ever played a game that used a spinner. When the spinner stopped, wherever the pointer landed indicated the player's next move (such as move ahead three spaces, collect $20, go to the red circle). We, too, have different options available to us, but in this case, *they* control the spinner; it stops where they want it to stop.

5. Distribute Worksheet 10-1.

6. Direct students' attention to the "Know This" box. Have a student volunteer read the sentence and inform students that they will need to know and understand this.

7. Direct students' attention to the "Try This" section. Call on a student volunteer to read the directions. Have students complete the activity by filling in the choice circles with behavior options.

8. When students have completed the activity, call on volunteers to supply behaviors for each example and discuss the appropriateness of the behaviors.

9. Have students complete the missing word from the "Review" section at the bottom of the worksheet.

> Most of the time, you can (choose) what behavior you want to happen.

10. ASSIGNMENT: Inform students that they will have a brief quiz tomorrow on the information covered in this lesson. You will give them a situation to consider, and they will be expected to supply four alternative behaviors and choose one that would be most appropriate for the situation.

11. Tell students to file Worksheet 10-1 in their folders.

THE CHOICE IS YOURS

> *Know This:* Most of the time, you can *choose* what behavior you want to happen.

Try This: What are some choices of behavior in each of the following situations? One example is given for you. Write in three more choices, then circle the choice you would pick. Why?

1. You are in a hurry to get to class, but your locker won't open.

   _____

   _____

   _____

   ask a friend to help

2. You and your best friend had an argument and you see him or her coming down the hall.

   _____

   _____

   _____

   ignore him

3. You didn't bother to study for the history test, but that didn't stop your teacher from giving you a test.

   _____

   _____

   _____

   tell him you feel sick

4. A new kid in your gym glass says that you can't hit the broad side of a barn.

   _____

   _____

   _____

   hit him

Review:

Most of the time, you can _____ what behavior you want to happen.

Lesson 11   CONSEQUENCES—WHAT HAPPENS NEXT

Overview

In this lesson, students are taught that a consequence is what happens because of a behavior that was chosen in a situation. In many cases, the consequence is another behavior. For example, if a student hits another student, the consequence might be getting hit back. In a later lesson, students will evaluate whether consequences are good (positive) or bad (negative) in preparation for choosing behaviors that will ultimately lead to attaining a goal. If a student's goal is to get attention from the teacher, then hitting another student may lead to a welcome consequence—sitting in the teacher's room after school. If the student's real goal, however, is to be accepted by other kids in the class, then hitting another student may not be the most appropriate behavior to reach that goal. The purpose of this lesson is to provide the students with practice in thinking ahead of a behavior to determine what the possible consequences might be.

Lesson Objective

- Students will identify one likely consequence of a given behavior.

Teacher Preparation

1. Make enough copies of Worksheet 11-1, "Consequences—What Happens Next," for your students.

2. Copy the following on the chalkboard:

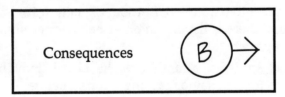

Lesson Plan

1. Review yesterday's lesson by stating that they talked about *choices.* Ask students to assist in summarizing the content of the lesson (for example, most of the time, you can choose what behavior you want to occur in a situation).

2. QUIZ: Inform students that, as promised, they will have a brief quiz to make sure they understand the idea of having choices of behavior in a situation. The situation they are to consider is (or you may want to supply your own):

> There is a substitute in your English class. You don't have your assignment done for the day. The substitute tells the class to pass forward their papers.

Answers may include: explain to the substitute that your work isn't done, ask if you can have more time, copy quickly from another student, hand in a blank piece of paper, hand in the wrong English assignment, quickly try to get the assignment done, and so on.

3. Collect the quizzes and discuss students' ideas for this situation.

4. Introduce today's lesson by directing students' attention to the chalkboard. Inform them that you will be talking about consequences of behaviors. This is defined as "A consequence is what happens because of a behavior." It may help students to think: "What might happen next?" Discuss these examples with students. What might happen next if

   a. someone came and hit you on the back? (you might hit that person)

   b. someone waves to you? (you might wave back)

   c. you study for five hours for a test? (you might pass)

   d. you practice shooting baskets all summer? (you might make the basketball team)

   e. you forget to deliver the newspapers on your route? (you might lose your job)

5. Distribute Worksheet 11-1.

6. Direct students' attention to the "Know This" box. Call on a student volunteer to read the definition. Explain to students that after a behavior occurs, there is usually another behavior or situation directly related to that behavior.

7. Direct students' attention to the board. Explain that the ⓑ→ symbol stands for a behavior causing a consequence. This information is also on their worksheet. You may want to go through a few examples such as those in step 4 to indicate the relationship between the behavior and the consequence.

8. Direct students' attention to the "Try This" section on their worksheet. Call on student volunteers to read the directions and the items. Have students complete the activity independently if desired and discuss their responses. At this point, only one consequence is required. It should be a logical consequence, if not entirely an appropriate one.

9. Have students complete the "Review" section at the bottom of the worksheet.

    > Sometimes there is a (better) time or place for a behavior to happen.
    >
    > Most of the time, you can (choose) what behavior you want to happen.

10. ASSIGNMENT: Inform students that as they go through the rest of their classes, be aware of what consequences they notice occurring because of their behavior. Each student should be prepared to cite at least one example of a behavior they chose to do and the consequence that occurred because of it. This assignment could be in writing if you wish.

11. Tell students to file Worksheet 11-1 in their folders.

CONSEQUENCES—WHAT HAPPENS NEXT

> *Know This:* A *consequence* is what happens because of a behavior. (Think: What might happen next?)

The behavior . . . (B) → causes a consequence.

Try This: Read each behavior below. Then give one consequence that could occur because of that behavior.

Behavior	A Consequence
1. You finished all your homework at school.	_____
2. You forgot to turn in your history assignment on time.	_____
3. You pressed too hard on your pencil during a math test.	_____
4. Your locker wouldn't open, so you kicked it as hard as you could.	_____
5. You left study hall in a hurry and forgot to get your books.	_____

What!!?? No homework again?

> *Review:*
>
> Sometimes there is a _____ time or place for a behavior to happen.
>
> Most of the time, you can _____ what behavior you want to happen.
>
> A _____ is what happens because of a behavior.

Lesson 12   MORE THAN ONE CONSEQUENCE

Overview

Now that students are familiar with the idea of a behavior causing a consequence, this idea is expanded to include multiple consequences. In different situations, the same behavior may produce very different consequences. For example, tapping someone on the back may evoke a teasing pat in return, a slap in the face, a call to the teacher, a threat of bodily harm, or laughter. Students need to be aware that a single behavior, coupled with a specific situation (as well as other variables), can cause any of a number of consequences. This lesson provides the student with practice in thinking of more than one consequence for a behavior.

Lesson Objective

● Students will state at least two plausible consequences for a given behavior.

Teacher Preparation

1. Make enough copies of Worksheet 12-1, "More than One Consequence," for your students.

2. Copy the following on the chalkboard:

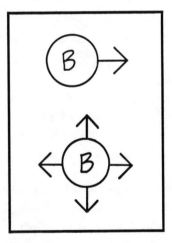

Lesson Plan

1. Review yesterday's lesson by asking students for examples of consequences that they observed in their classes that were a result of behaviors they engaged in.

2. Direct students' attention to the board. Ask for a student volunteer to explain the meaning of the first symbol (a behavior causes a consequence).

3. Distribute Worksheet 12-1.

4. Direct students' attention to the "Know This" box. Ask for a student volunteer to read the definition.

5. Explain to students that the same behavior may cause very different consequences, depending on the situation. This is something they should be aware of when they decide what behavior they are going to do. They will need to practice "thinking ahead" before they find themselves in a consequence that was not what they had intended.

6. Direct students' attention to the second symbol on the board. Explain that this shows that the same behavior might cause one of several different consequences. For example,

   a. yelling in the middle of class
      ● the teacher might have you write sentences
      ● you might have to stay after class
      ● the girl in front of you might turn around and tell you to be quiet
      ● the boy behind you might yell at you to quit being so loud

   b. sleeping on the bus
      ● you might miss your stop
      ● you might not get the homework done that you usually do on the bus
      ● you might not sleep at night
      ● you might snore and disturb the person next to you

7. Direct students' attention to the "Try This" section. Call on a student volunteer to read the directions. Inform students that they are to complete the consequence chart by supplying possible consequences for each behavior. Have students complete the activity independently or in small groups and discuss their responses. Answers may include

---

1. Have to pay for the book, miss assignments, spend time looking for the book instead of doing your class work.

2. Have to spend extra time studying math, spend time after school making up work or tests, not get to play on the basketball team.

3. Not be able to do your assignments in science, get in trouble with teacher or parents for trying to destroy school property, have to pay for another book.

---

8. Have students complete the "Review" section at the bottom of the worksheet.

> A (consequence) is what happens because of a behavior.
>
> A behavior may have (more) than one consequence.

9. ASSIGNMENT: In preparation for tomorrow's lesson, have students be ready to provide at least three possible consequences for the following behavior(s):

   a. doing sloppy work on a writing assignment

   b. arguing with the teacher about a test

   c. slamming a door loudly

   You might want to have students select one of the three behaviors and have the assignment in writing.

10. Tell students to file Worksheet 12-1 in their folders.

MORE THAN ONE CONSEQUENCE

Know This: A behavior may have *more* than one consequence.

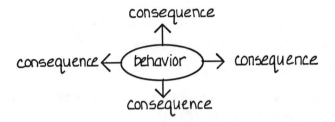

Try This: Read each behavior below. One possible consequence is given. Complete each chart by filling in three other consequences that could occur because of the behavior.

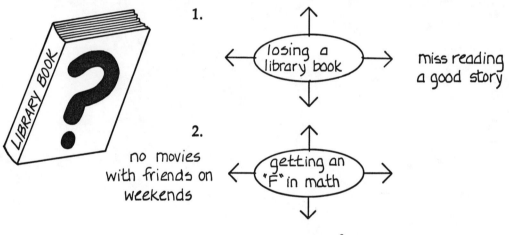

1. losing a library book → miss reading a good story

2. getting an "F" in math ← no movies with friends on weekends

3. you have to pay for damages ← throwing your science book in the trash

---

Review:

A _____ is what happens because of a behavior.

A behavior may have _____ than one consequence.

Lesson 13   GOOD AND BAD CONSEQUENCES

Overview

Categorizing consequences into good, bad, or even neutral classes can be a rather complex task since it is very much dependent on the point of view of the behavior. Getting attention from someone by displaying inappropriate behavior in a situation may be a "good" consequence. However, since the attention may be unpleasant (a reprimand, for example, or a scowl), this could also be an unpleasant or "bad" consequence. The purpose of this lesson is to give students practice in viewing a situation and consequence as "good" (if it gets you something you want) and "bad" (if it may not be the best way to get what you want). Some of the exercises may require a bit of thinking to come up with both good and bad aspects of a consequence. The point is that students realize no situation is completely good or bad; there are good and bad aspects of every behavior. This lesson is, of course, a very simplistic way of dealing with a complex idea. The ideas of rightness, wrongness, values, and moral judgments are beyond the scope of this lesson. The student is only expected to see two sides of the behavior and consequence.

Lesson Objective

- Given a behavior, the students will state one good or positive consequence and one bad or negative consequence of that behavior.

Teacher Preparation

Make enough copies of Worksheet 13-1, "Good and Bad Consequences," for your students.

Lesson Plan

1. Review yesterday's lesson by discussing three possible consequences for each of the following behaviors:

   a. doing sloppy work on a writing assignment
      - having to redo the assignment
      - getting a lower grade on the assignment
      - having the teacher comment that you are not working up to ability
   b. arguing with the teacher about a test
      - other students will get into the argument, too

47

- the teacher might get upset and send you to the principal
- you will get yourself upset and not do well on other tests

c. slamming a door loudly

- the teacher will embarrass you by asking you not to be so rude
- other students will laugh at you
- you'll get attention from other students because you were loud

2. Introduce today's lesson by informing students that you will be looking more closely at the consequences of a behavior and deciding if they are good or bad consequences. Ask students for ideas of what "good" and "bad" consequences might mean. (Responses may include if it gets you in trouble, it's bad, but if it doesn't get you in trouble, it's good; "good" might mean you got what you wanted out of the situation.)

3. Distribute Worksheet 13-1.

4. Direct students' attention to the "Know This" box. Call on a student volunteer to read the definition.

5. Explain the example to students. Eating spinach is a behavior—one possible consequence is that your health has been improved, which could be thought of as a "good" consequence. Alternatively, if you don't care for the taste of spinach, the taste left in your mouth may be an unpleasant consequence.

6. For extra practice in classifying consequences as good or bad, discuss the following behaviors and consequences orally. Have students decide whether the consequence is a good one or a bad one.

a. untying your shoe—tripping (bad consequence)

b. eating your vegetable—getting an extra dessert from your mother (good consequence)

c. babysitting for your little sister—getting $5 (good consequence)

d. watching TV instead of studying—getting a D on the test (bad consequence)

e. forgetting to cut the grass—losing your allowance (bad consequence)

f. brushing your teeth—having no cavities (good consequence)

g. knocking over your milk—having to mop the floor (bad consequence)

h. waving to a friend—the friend comes to sit by you (good consequence)

i. lending a friend some money—the friend never pays you back (bad consequence)

j. putting money in a candy machine—getting a candy bar (good consequence)

k. putting money in a candy machine—losing your money (bad consequence)

7. Direct students' attention to the "Try This" section of the worksheet. Call on student volunteers to read the directions and the items. You may want to have students write their responses or discuss items orally in class. Suggested answers are given with the good consequence first, followed by the bad consequence:

---

1. You will be able to find everything./It takes a long time.
2. You can go out with friends on Saturday./You might miss going out with friends on Friday.
3. You may get a better grade./You may have to miss something fun to redo the assignment.
4. You will get better at playing the piano./You will be frustrated at all the mistakes you make.
5. Your mother will be happy./You hate to drag the trash bags across the yard in front of all your friends.
6. A friend might share his dessert with you next time./You won't get as much of the dessert this time.
7. You might get paid for babysitting./You will miss the fun of practicing with your team.

---

8. Have students complete the "Review" section at the bottom of the worksheet.

   A (consequence) is what happens because of a behavior.

   A behavior may have (more) than one consequence.

   Consequences of a behavior can be (good) or (bad).

9. ASSIGNMENT: Ask students to be prepared to give one behavior that they have observed or done themselves in school and state one good consequence and one bad consequence of that behavior.

10. Tell students to file Worksheet 13-1 in their folders.

GOOD AND BAD CONSEQUENCES

Know This: Consequences of a behavior can be *good* or *bad*.

it's probably
very good
for my health   ← eating spinach →   it leaves an
awful taste in
my mouth

Try This: Think about each behavior below. Can you think of a good consequence AND a bad consequence for each?

Behavior	Good	Bad
1. Cleaning out your desk	_____ _____	_____ _____
2. Doing homework Friday night	_____ _____	_____ _____
3. Recopying a messy assignment	_____ _____	_____ _____
4. Practicing the piano	_____ _____	_____ _____
5. Taking out the garbage	_____ _____	_____ _____
6. Sharing your dessert with a friend	_____ _____	_____ _____
7. Missing basketball practice to babysit your little sister	_____ _____	_____ _____

Review:

A _____ is what happens because of a behavior.

A behavior may have _____ than one consequence.

Consequences of a behavior can be _____ or _____.

Lesson 14   SETTING A GOAL

Overview

Whether students are conscious of it or not, most behavior is goal directed. The things that people do have reasons behind them—usually a motive to "get" something or "be" something. This lesson introduces students to the idea that a behavior is performed in order to get closer to a goal. It also introduces the idea of goal setting: choosing the goal *before* the behavior is performed.

Lesson Objectives

- Students will identify a possible goal for a given behavior.
- Students will identify the most appropriate behavior to attain a given goal.

Teacher Preparation

1. Make enough copies of Worksheet 14-1, "Setting a Goal: Reach for the Stars," and Worksheet 14-2, "A Boy and His Dog," for your students.

2. Copy the following on the chalkboard:

Setting a Goal

Lesson Plan

1. Review yesterday's lesson by asking students to give an example of one behavior that they had observed in school and state one good consequence and one bad consequence of that behavior.

2. Introduce today's lesson by stating students will be learning about setting a goal and how their behavior affects their goals.

3. Direct students' attention to the board. Explain that the star symbol will be used to indicate setting or reaching a goal. They may associate this with the idea of reaching for something far off, but attractive and identifiable.

4. Explain that when a person behaves in a certain way, he or she is really working toward reaching a goal—whether that person knows what that

goal is or not. Behaviors are done for a reason, and if you stop to think about it, you usually can figure out what that reason (goal) is.

5. Discuss the following examples:

   a. What are some reasons for brushing your teeth?
      - not wanting to get cavities
      - wanting your breath to feel fresh
      - wanting whiter teeth
      - wanting your mother to quit nagging you about brushing

   b. What are some reasons for practicing spelling words?
      - wanting to pass the spelling test
      - wanting your teacher to be proud of you
      - not wanting to write missed words ten times

6. Conclude that the same behavior—brushing teeth, practicing spelling words—may have different goals for different people.

7. Distribute Worksheet 14-1.

8. Direct students' attention to the "Know This" box. Call on student volunteers to read the sentences. Emphasize the words "want" and "reach."

9. Direct students' attention to the "Try This" section. Call on a student volunteer to read the directions. You may want to have the class do this activity orally, since the second worksheet involves written responses. Answers may include

   1. I want to get 100% on the test Friday.
   2. I want to get dessert.
   3. I want to make the track team.
   4. I want to be able to find my missing math book.
   5. I want to borrow Dad's car this weekend.
   6. I want to finish this book before it is due.
   7. I want to get a good grade on the assignment.
   8. I want to remember all of my homework.
   9. I want to wear the sweatshirt on Friday.
   10. I want to borrow my sister's coat.

10. Summarize the activity for students by concluding that most goals could start with "I want . . ." something.

11. Distribute Worksheet 14-2.

12. Explain to students that the boy's goal in this activity is to get a dog. The obstacle seems to be the boy's father, so the boy is trying to convince his dad that he should have a dog. Two approaches are shown. Students are to analyze the two approaches to see which one is more likely to lead the boy to his goal.

13. Call on student volunteers to read the "Behavior" and "Consequence" sections of Situation A and Situation B.

14. Direct students' attention to the "Questions" section of the worksheet. Have students complete the activity independently before coming together as a group to discuss the responses. Answers are

---

1. To get a dog.
2. To get a dog.
3. Forgot to feed cats.
4. Fed the neighbor's dog.
5. A—dad doesn't trust him; B—dad takes him seriously.
6. No.
7. Bad.
8. Yes.
9. Good.
10. Yes.
11. Choosing behavior in Situation B brought him closer to his goal.
12. Situation B.

---

15. Direct students' attention to the "Review" box. Have students complete the missing words.

Setting a goal means deciding what you (want).

Your behavior helps you (reach) your goal.

16. ASSIGNMENT: Have students select one goal related to school that they would really like to attain. They should also think of at least one behavior they could do that would help them reach that goal. You may want to have students prepare this assignment in writing.

17. Tell students to file Worksheets 14-1 and 14-2 in their folders.

SETTING A GOAL: REACH FOR THE STARS

> *Know This:* Setting a goal means deciding what you *want*.
> Your behavior helps you *reach* your goal.

Try This: These students are talking about a behavior they are going to do. Decide what is the goal for each student. (Think: What do they really want? Why are they doing that behavior?) The first one has been done to help you get started.

Behavior	Goal ☆
1. I'm going to practice my spelling words every night.	I want to get 100% on the test Friday.
2. I'm going to eat everything on my plate at dinner tonight.	
3. I'm going to run around the track five times without stopping.	
4. I'm going to clean out my locker at school.	
5. I'm going to wash my dad's car.	
6. I'm going to read one story in this book every night.	
7. I'm going to check over this English assignment to make sure everything is spelled correctly.	
8. I'm going to write down all my homework assignments on a piece of paper.	
9. I'm going to wash my favorite sweatshirt before the party on Friday.	
10. I'm going to be nice to my sister.	

SETTING A GOAL: A BOY AND HIS DOG

Goal: I want my dad to let me have a dog.

SITUATION A

Behavior: I forget to feed my cats a couple of times.

Consequence: Dad tells me I don't take good care of the pets I've got, so forget about a dog.

SITUATION B

Behavior: I feed the neighbor's dog while the family is on vacation for two weeks.

Consequence: Dad sees that I really mean it about wanting a dog and being able to take care of one, so he is more likely to let me have one.

Questions

1. What is the boy's goal in Situation A? _____

2. What is the boy's goal in Situation B? _____

3. What was his behavior like in A? _____

4. What was his behavior like in B? _____

5. What kind of consequence resulted from the behavior in A? _____

   _____ in B? _____

   _____

6. Did the consequence in A get him closer to his goal? _____

7. Was that consequence good or bad for the boy? _____

8. Did the consequence in B get him closer to his goal? _____

9. Was that consequence good or bad for the boy? _____

10. Did the boy have a choice of behaviors? _____

11. How did his choice affect the consequences? _____

    _____

12. Which behavior was the best one for him to do? _____

    _____

Review:
Setting a goal means deciding what you _____.

Your behavior helps you _____ your goal.

Lesson 15   MAKING A PLAN

Overview

Once students have a goal in mind, something they want, they need to devise a plan to reach that goal. Often the biggest obstacle to reaching a goal is not systematically deciding *how* you are actually, practically, realistically going to get there. Some guidelines are given to students for making a plan, and students are asked to evaluate several plans as they relate to goals. A ladder symbol is used to represent the process of making a plan. This helps to convey the idea that reaching a goal might be a "one-step-at-a-time" process, getting ever closer to that goal.

Lesson Objectives

- Students will evaluate plans for given goals as to their sensibility and practicality.
- Students will devise a plan to reach a goal (selected from Lesson 14).

Teacher Preparation

1. Make enough copies of Worksheet 15-1, "Making a Plan," for your students.
2. Copy the following on the chalkboard:

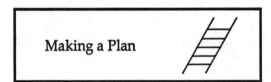

Lesson Plan

1. Review yesterday's lesson by having students state or produce in writing a school-related goal they would like to attain. Ask for student volunteers to share their goals.
2. Introduce today's lesson by stating that the first step to take after setting a goal is to make a plan to reach that goal. It's not going to happen by itself—they have to *make* it happen.
3. Direct students' attention to the board. Ask students for ideas why a ladder may be a good symbol to represent the attempt to reach a goal. (Ideas may include taking steps toward reaching something far off.)

4. Distribute Worksheet 15-1.

5. Direct students' attention to the "Know This" box. Call on student volunteers to read the sentence and the two guidelines for making a plan.

6. Discuss why the examples would not make good plans. Answers may include

   a. First example
      - does not make sense
      - eating cake probably does not have much to do with passing the class
   b. Second example
      - is not realistic
      - brushing teeth is a much more appropriate way to avoid cavities

7. Direct students' attention to the "Try This" section. Call on student volunteers to read the goals and corresponding plans. Discuss what makes the plans appropriate or not appropriate. Answers may include

   ---
   1. BAD PLAN—It is not realistic to write each word 1,000 times a night.
   2. GOOD PLAN—It is sensible and realistic.
   3. BAD PLAN—Writing assignments on paper makes more sense than writing them on a shirt sleeve.
   ---

8. Draw students' attention to the "Review" section and have them complete the sentences.

   Setting a goal means deciding what you (want).

   Your behavior helps you (reach) your goal.

   Making a plan is deciding (how) you are going to reach your goal.

9. ASSIGNMENT: Ask students to look again at the goals they have chosen to work on at school for Lesson 14. Assign students the project of devising a workable, sensible plan to reach that goal. Plans do not have to be elaborate at this point, but should reflect a logical approach to the goal. You may want to have students put their ideas in writing. Inform students that their ideas will be discussed in class on a volunteer basis so as not to embarrass any students who may have personal goals they do not want to share.

10. Tell students to file Worksheet 15-1 in their folders.

Name _____ Date _____

MAKING A PLAN

Know This: Making a plan is deciding *how* you are going to reach your goal.

Your plan has to *make sense.*

> I want to pass my home economics class, so I'm going to eat cake 5 times a day!

Your plan has to be *realistic.*

> I don't want cavities, so I'll pull out all of my teeth!

Try This: What do you think of these plans?

1. My goal is to get an "A" on the spelling test.
   My plan is to write each word 1,000 times every night.

   _____

   _____

   _____

2. My goal is to have a clean desk.
   My plan is to empty it completely, throw out all the trash, and put my books in order.

   _____

   _____

   _____

3. My goal is to write down all of my assignments.
   My plan is to write them down right away on my shirt sleeve so I'll know where they are.

   _____

   _____

   _____

Review:

Setting a goal means deciding what you _____.

Your behavior helps you _____ your goal.

Making a plan is deciding _____ you are going to reach your goal.

Lesson 16 KEEPING TRACK OF YOUR BEHAVIOR

Overview

The most realistic goals and well-intentioned plans will not be beneficial to students if they are not carried out. By documenting the efforts, students will find that they are accountable for their behavior—either to the teacher or (eventually) to themselves. Flaws in plans will also be more apparent if the evidence is there in black and white for them to see. Is homework less likely to be finished on a Friday? Is it easier to raise your hand in math class than in English class? Often, the very act of monitoring one's behavior is enough to cause a change in that behavior. The purpose of this lesson is to familiarize students with three examples of behaviors, plans, and monitoring systems for the plans.

Lesson Objectives

- Students will identify whether or not a plan has been correctly carried out in given situations.
- Students will identify a possible monitoring system to carry out their plans for changing a school behavior.

Teacher Preparation

1. Make enough copies of Worksheet 16-1, "Keeping Track of Your Behavior: Recording Minutes," Worksheet 16-2, "Keeping Track of Your Behavior: Using a Tally Sheet," and Worksheet 16-3, "Keeping Track of Your Behavior: Using a Yes/No Chart," for your students. You might want to collate and assemble these worksheets into one packet for each student.

2. Copy the following on the chalkboard:

> Keeping Track of Your Behavior

Lesson Plan

1. Review yesterday's material by asking student volunteers to share their plans for their goals. Discuss briefly among the class whether or not the plans shared appear to be workable and sensible.

2. Introduce today's lesson by stating that the next consideration for their plans is finding a way to keep track of their behavior. Ask for ideas of why this may be important, such as you don't want to forget what your original goal is, it might help you to remember what to do each day, it will help you see if things are changing or not.

3. Direct students' attention to the board. Explain that the pencil symbol indicates keeping track of a behavior.

4. Distribute Worksheets 16-1 through 16-3.

5. Explain to students that they will be looking at three examples of student plans to reach a goal and three different ways of keeping track of a behavior.

6. Direct students' attention to the "Know This" box of Worksheet 16-1. Ask for a student volunteer to read the sentence. Reiterate why it is important to keep track of a behavior.

7. Ask for student volunteers to read the comments made by the first student-model, Nancy.

8. Explain that Nancy used a card to keep track of her behavior. Ask students what information was recorded in the first column (day of the week), second column (times spent studying her social studies), and third column (total number of minutes spent studying).

9. Direct students' attention to the "Try This" section of the first page. Briefly discuss the questions as a class and allow time for comments as to the workability of this plan. Answers are

> 1. Yes.
> 2. No.
> 3. She forgot (but give her credit for her honesty).
> 4. Yes.
> 5. Yes, she followed her plan 80% of the time (four out of five days).

10. Direct students' attention to Worksheet 16-2.

11. Ask for student volunteers to read the comments made by this student-model, Paul.

12. Explain that Paul also used a card to keep track of his behavior, but his recording system only involved making a tally mark each time the behavior occurred.

13. Direct students' attention to the "Try This" section. Briefly discuss the questions as a class and allow time for comments as to the workability of this plan. Answers are

> 1. Yes.
> 2. Two.
> 3. No.
> 4. Yes.
> 5. There was a test—probably no opportunity to raise his hand to answer a question.
> 6. Try it for a longer time—he really didn't have enough of a chance to give it a try (four days).

14. Direct students' attention to Worksheet 16-3.

15. Ask for student volunteers to read the comments made by this student-model, Claudia.

16. Explain that Claudia used a card to keep track of her behavior also, but her recording system was just to write *yes* or *no* according to whether or not the plan was used.

17. Direct students' attention to the "Try This" section of the worksheet. Briefly discuss the questions as a class and allow time for comments as to the workability of this plan. Answers are

> 1. Yes.
> 2. Yes.
> 3. No.
> 4. A snowstorm prevented her from going to the library.
> 5. Yes (if not for the snowstorm, she would have had 100% success with this plan).

18. Direct students' attention to the "Review" sentences Have students complete the missing words.

Setting a goal means deciding what you (want).

Your behavior helps you (reach) your goal.

Making a plan is deciding (how) you are going to reach your goals.

You can tell if your plans are working by keeping (track) of your behavior.

19. ASSIGNMENTS: Keeping students' personal goal and plan in mind, students should be prepared to offer a plan for keeping track of their behavior. Inform students that you will ask for student volunteers to share their plans during the next lesson. Also inform students that they should expect a brief quiz on the review statements from Lessons 14–16. The review statements appear on Worksheet 16-3.

20. Tell students to file Worksheets 16-1 through 16-3 in their folders.

Name _____ Date _____

KEEPING TRACK OF YOUR BEHAVIOR: RECORDING MINUTES

> *Know This:* You can tell if your plan is working by keeping *track* of your behavior.

How is Nancy doing?

My goal is to get a "B" in social studies.

My plan is to study my social studies for 20 minutes every night.

I will keep track of this behavior (studying) by writing down my times every night. See?

Mon.	7:00–7:20	20 minutes
Tues.	8:00–8:25	25 minutes
Wed.	forgot	
Thurs.	6:00–6:20	20 minutes
Fri.	6:30–6:55	25 minutes

Try This:

1. Did Nancy follow her plan on Monday? _____

2. Did she follow her plan on Wednesday? _____

3. What happened on Wednesday? _____

4. Did Nancy follow her plan on Thursday and Friday? _____

5. Do you think this plan is working for Nancy? _____

KEEPING TRACK OF YOUR BEHAVIOR: USING A TALLY SHEET

How is Paul doing?

My <u>goal</u> is to answer more questions in science class.
My <u>plan</u> is to raise my hand to answer the teacher's questions at least 3 times every class period.
I will keep <u>track</u> of this behavior (raising my hand) by putting a mark on a piece of paper every time I raise my hand.

Mon.	////
Tue.	//
Wed.	/
Thurs.	////
Fri.	(test)

Try This:

1. Did Paul follow his plan on Monday? _____

2. How many times did Paul raise his hand on Tuesday? _____

3. Did Paul follow his plan on Wednesday? _____

4. Did he follow his plan on Thursday? _____

5. What happened on Friday? _____

6. Do you think he should try this plan longer or stop? _____

Name _____ Date _____

KEEPING TRACK OF YOUR BEHAVIOR: USING A YES/NO CHART

How is Claudia doing?

My <u>goal</u> is to read 4 library books every week.

My <u>plan</u> is to go to the library every Friday and check out 4 books and return them (read, of course) the next Friday.

I will keep <u>track</u> of this behavior (reading books) by writing YES or NO next to the date of each Friday.

Week of 1/15	YES
Week of 1/22	YES
Week of 1/29	YES
Week of 2/5	YES
Week of 2/12	NO (snowstorm)

Try This:

1. Did Claudia follow her plan the first week? _____

2. Did she follow her plan the week of 2/5? _____

3. Did she follow her plan the week of 2/12? _____

4. What happened on the 2/12 week? _____

5. Do you think this plan is working for Claudia? _____

Review:

Setting a goal means deciding what you _____.

Your behavior helps you _____ your goal.

Making a plan is deciding _____ you are going to reach your goal.

You can tell if your plan is working by keeping _____ of your behavior.

Lesson 17   REWARDING YOURSELF

Overview

This lesson introduces the student to the idea of rewarding himself for his accomplishments. Most students are probably used to the idea of receiving some type of reward for performing a task, such as money for doing chores or getting good grades, a social reinforcement like a pat on the back for doing something that someone else approved of, or a special activity (field trip, class party) for good group performance. The student, however, can also be the agent that provides the reward for himself. He is the one who knows what he will work for, after all! The purpose of this lesson is to familiarize the student with several different types of rewards, examples of self-rewards, and to give the student an opportunity to evaluate several rewards to determine which ones would be interesting or appropriate for him to consider.

Lesson Objectives

- Students will identify appropriate rewards for typical school situations.
- Students will specify at least two appropriate self-rewards.

Teacher Preparation

1. Make enough copies of Worksheet 17-1, "Rewarding Yourself: Examples of Rewards," Worksheet 17-2, "Rewarding Yourself: Let's Be Realistic," and Worksheet 17-3, "Rewarding Yourself: Give This a Try," for your students. You might want to collate and assemble the three worksheets into one packet.

2. Copy the following on the chalkboard:

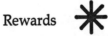

Rewards

1. Tangible (something you can see or hold)
2. Social (other people)
3. Activity (something to do)

3. Prepare for the students' quiz by writing the following statements either on the chalkboard or on a ditto:

QUIZ

1. Setting a goal means deciding what you _____.
2. Your behavior helps you _____ your goal.
3. Making a plan is deciding _____ you are going to reach your goal.
4. You can tell if your plan is working by keeping _____ of your behavior.

Answers in order are "want," "reach," "how," and "track."

Lesson Plan

1. Inform students that they have a quiz, as promised, on the review statements of the last three lessons. Distribute the quiz or direct students' attention to the board containing the statements.
2. Collect the quizzes and briefly discuss the correct answers.
3. Review yesterday's material by asking student volunteers to share their ideas for appropriate plans to keep track of targeted behaviors. You may want to list some of their ideas on the board. Discuss the workability of the plans.
4. Introduce today's lesson by stating that the students are going to be thinking about rewards and rewarding themselves for good work.
5. Direct students' attention to the board. Explain that the symbol will be used to indicate a reward. It is similar in some ways to the star (goal) symbol in that they both represent something good. Mention that there are many different kinds of rewards. Briefly explain:

   a. A *tangible* reward is something that can be seen or held, such as money, food, a movie pass.

   b. A *social* reward is something that involves other people, such as a smile, a pat on the back.

   c. An *activity* reward is something you do, such as going roller skating, having free time.

   Mention that there will be overlap among rewards. For example, roller skating with your best friend might be both a social and activity reward.
6. Distribute Worksheets 17-1 through 17-3.

7. Direct students' attention to Worksheet 17-1. Have a student volunteer read the "Know This" comment. Ask students why it is important to reward yourself *after* you have accomplished something, rather than before. (Example: You will want to make sure you really carry through on your plan.)

8. Call on student volunteers to read the examples on the worksheet. As each is read, ask students to categorize the reward into one of three example reward groups (tangible, social, or activity) and explain why. Answers are

> A. Tangible (money) possibly social (praise from dad)
> B. Social (praise and pat on the back)
> C. Tangible (food)
> D. Social (a kiss)
> E. Activity (listening to the radio)

9. Direct students' attention to Worksheet 17-2. Explain that there are ways to reward yourself for your accomplishments. Discuss briefly why this may be necessary or better than having other people do the rewarding. (Examples: You know yourself better than other people, so you know what rewards would be good for you; other people may not be around, so there would be no one to reward you.)

10. Call on student volunteers to read the first three examples and briefly discuss the types of self-rewards that are shown. Answers are

> A. Activity (watching television)
> B. Social (visiting with friends) or activity (going to the park)
> C. Tangible (food)

11. Call attention to example D on the worksheet. Explain that a reward has to be realistic. Ask for student comments about the example.

12. Direct students' attention to Worksheet 17-3. Have a student volunteer read the directions and discuss the items on the list. You may want to

have students complete the inventory independently and then come together as a group to discuss the responses. Suggested answers are

```
      1.  + (easy to do, accessible)
      2.  + (if you have the money)
      3.  (unrealistic for most of us)
      4.  + (accessible)
      5.  (unrealistic)
      6.  (might be gratifying, but not really appropriate)
      7.  + (probably accessible)
      8.  + (comic books, library book)
      9.  + (probably accessible to most people)
     10.  (unrealistic)
     11.  + (easy, accessible)
     12.  + (if done at the proper time)
     13.  (probably subject to parental approval)
     14.  + (good social reward)
     15.  (unrealistic)
```

13. Direct students' attention to the "Review" box. Call on a student volunteer to read the statement. Have students complete the missing words.

    After you have done a good job on your plan, you can (reward) yourself.

14. ASSIGNMENT: Inform students that for tomorrow's class, you would like them to have a list of at least two possible appropriate rewards that are accessible to them for rewarding themselves. You may want to have students classify the rewards into one of the three types discussed in this lesson (tangible, social, activity).

15. Tell students to file Worksheets 17-1 through 17-3 in their folders.

REWARDING YOURSELF: EXAMPLES OF REWARDS

Know This: After you have done a good job on your plan, you can *reward* yourself.

Examples of rewards:

A.

B.

C.

D.

E.

REWARDING YOURSELF:
LET'S BE REALISTIC

Examples of rewarding yourself:

A.

I know this math is hard, but when I'm done, I'll reward myself by watching T.V.!

B.

I really don't want to do this homework right away, but if I finish it quickly, I'll have time to go to the park with my friends.

C.

I hate looking up words to make sure they're spelled right, but I'll reward myself by getting a hot fudge sundae when I'm done.

D. Your reward has to be something you can really *get* or *do*.

I think I deserve a pony!

You might deserve one, but you might not get one!!!

REWARDING YOURSELF:
GIVE THIS A TRY

Try This:

Think about these rewards. Which ones might be good ones to reward yourself? Put a + in front of the ones that you think might be good. What might be a problem with some of them?

_____ 1. Going out with a friend

_____ 2. Buying a new record

_____ 3. Going on a vacation to the Bahamas

_____ 4. Eating an ice cream cone

_____ 5. Skipping school for a week

_____ 6. Hitting your little brother

_____ 7. Playing videogames

_____ 8. Reading something good

_____ 9. Watching TV

_____ 10. Buying yourself a car

_____ 11. Listening to the radio

_____ 12. Daydreaming

_____ 13. Buying yourself a St. Bernard puppy

_____ 14. Spending time with someone you like

_____ 15. Giving yourself $300,000

Review:
After you have done a good job on your plan, you can _____ yourself.

Lesson 18   EVALUATION—HOW DID I DO?

Overview

The ultimate test of any plan is whether or not it results in reaching the desired goal through lasting changes in one's behavior. Looking at this from a long-term perspective can help to eliminate the frustration of temporary setbacks in behavior. There are going to be ups and downs with any type of program, but as long as the student realizes that he or she is making progress toward a goal, the student should feel successful. Change takes *time* as well as commitment. The evaluation process is one that can help the student objectively look at where she is going and how far she has come. If the student has not reached the goal she has set for herself within the amount of time she has allocated, there are several areas to consider: Is she adhering to the plan? Is her plan a reasonable one? Is her goal unattainable? Is she lacking motivation to continue the project? Does she just need some moral support? Stopping to evaluate her plan, goal, and behavior carefully is a crucial step for the student. Not only is it a learning experience to pinpoint weaknesses in the current project and remedy them, it is also very gratifying for the student to experience firsthand the success that comes with being in control of her own situation and self. The purpose of this lesson is to provide the student with questions that he or she is to ask himself or herself and consider in relation to his or her own project.

Lesson Objective

- Students will be able to state at least three evaluation questions that will be helpful in considering a plan.

Teacher Preparation

1. Make enough copies of Worksheet 18-1, "Evaluation—How Did I Do?," for your students.
2. Copy the following on the chalkboard:

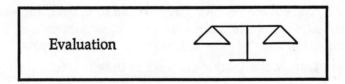

Lesson Plan

1. Review yesterday's material by asking students to give examples of a tangible reward, a social reward, and an activity reward.

2. Continue the review by asking student volunteers to share their lists of at least two personal rewards they have chosen.

3. Introduce today's lesson by stating that the final, and a most important, step in making a plan to change behavior is that of evaluation. Ask students to give ideas as to why this would be important. (For example, lets you know if you have accomplished what you set out to do, lets you look at something objectively.)

4. Direct students' attention to the board. Explain that the scale or balance symbol will be used to indicate evaluation of a plan. Ask for ideas why the scale would be a good one to represent this process. (For example, conveys the idea of weighing alternatives, such as good versus bad or positive versus negative; perhaps some things were successful about the plan, but other parts offset the success.)

5. Distribute copies of Worksheet 18-1.

6. Direct students' attention to the "Know This" box. Call on student volunteers to read the statement and the two examples. Discuss briefly why the girl's plan in Example A probably is not a very good one (studying social studies did not help her math grades because one is not directly related to the other) and why the boy's plan in Example B was a good plan (an organized locker allowed more time for getting to class).

7. Direct students' attention to the "Questions" section. Call on student volunteers to read the questions listed. Explain that when students actually complete their projects, they will want to use these questions to help themselves evaluate what they did.

8. Direct students' attention to the "Review" box. Have students complete the missing word from the review statement.

    You should evaluate your plan to see if it is making a (difference) in your behavior.

9. ASSIGNMENT: Inform students that the next lesson is a review of all the material covered so far. They should look over the worksheets from all previous lessons to make sure they either understand the concepts or have questions ready to be discussed in class tomorrow.

10. Tell students to file Worksheet 18-1 in their folders.

EVALUATION—HOW DID I DO?

> *Know This:* You should evaluate your plan to see if it is making **a** *difference* in your behavior.

A.

Studying social studies every night is NOT helping me do better in math!

B.

This is interesting.....keeping my books organized in my locker is helping me get to class on time!

Questions:

If things don't seem to be working well, ask yourself:

1. Am I following my plan carefully?
2. Do I have everything I need to carry out my plan?
3. Is the plan too hard or too easy?
4. Is my goal too hard or too easy?
5. Do I need to change the reward?
6. Do other people have some helpful ideas?
7. Do I really want to change my behavior?

Well, I think...

Why don't you try.....

> *Review:*
>
> You should evaluate your plan to see if it is making a
>
> ———————————————— in your behavior.

Lesson 19 REVIEW LESSON—ALL ABOUT BEHAVIOR

Overview

The student has been given a lot of material and concepts to become familiar with. At this time, it is important to stop, review, and make sure that students really understand the specific points emphasized in each lesson and can grasp how they all fit together to form a coherent plan for change. The purpose of this lesson is to review systematically the major points covered in previous lessons and to provide the student with a problem-solving model that he or she can use to help formulate his or her own projects for behavior change.

Lesson Objectives

- Students will identify the major points of a problem-solving model.
- Students will demonstrate knowledge of basic concepts by stating review sentences, supplying missing words in definitions, or providing examples for given situations.

Teacher Preparation

Make enough copies of Worksheet 19-1, "Problem-Solving Model," and Worksheet 19-2, "Review," for your students. You might want to collate and assemble the two worksheets into a review guide.

Lesson Plan

1. Introduce today's lesson by informing students that they will spend class time reviewing all previous lesson worksheets and a problem-solving model worksheet.
2. Distribute Worksheet 19-1.
3. Call on student volunteers to read the various sections of the worksheet. Explain that this worksheet demonstrates how the various components of behavior they have been studying fit together and can be used to solve problems they may encounter in school.
4. Distribute Worksheet 19-2. (This is a multipage worksheet.)
5. You might want to have students work independently on this review packet. Students should use their previous worksheets (neatly assembled

in an orderly manner in their folders) to answer the questions. In some cases, the student is asked whether or not he or she understands the material on the worksheet. Instruct students to put a checkmark in the box next to each worksheet number on the review sheet to indicate that they understand the material. Here are suggested answers:

Worksheet 1-1

1. Answers will vary (may be labeled a troublemaker).
2. Answers will vary (acquire more freedom).

Worksheet 2-1

3. Good; could be better.
4. (Good) answers will vary (does homework, is prepared); (Could be better) answers will vary (sloppy worker, turns in late work).

Worksheets 3-1 and 3-2

5. Answers will vary.
6. Answers will vary.
7. Answers will vary.

Worksheet 4-1

8. You or yourself.
9. Effort.

Worksheet 5-1

10. Answers will vary.

Worksheet 6-1

11. Read lessons, take test.
12. Assist student, praise, ensure reward.
13. Answers will vary (see contract).
14. Answers will vary (see contract).
15. Answers will vary (see contract).

Worksheets 7-1 through 18-1

16. a. behavior; b. choices; c. consequences; d. goal; e. plan; f. keeping track of behavior; g. reward; h. evaluation.
17. a. do; b. places; c. better; d. choose; e. consequence; f. more; g. good/bad; h. want; i. reach; j. how; k. track; l. reward; m. difference.

Worksheet 7-1

18. Opinion.

19. Studying, running, talking, and so on.

Worksheet 8-1

20. Opinion.

21. Answers will vary (talking to a teacher, sitting at a desk taking a test).

Worksheet 9-1

22. Opinion.

23. Answers will vary (noisy, distracting, no place to put your books, etc.).

Worksheet 10-1

24. Opinion.

25. Answers will vary (laugh about it, cry, get up, ask for help, etc.).

Worksheet 11-1

26. Opinion.

27. Answers will vary (people might laugh at you).

Worksheet 12-1

28. Opinion.

29. Answers will vary (you might fall asleep during the test, you might oversleep and miss the bus, etc.).

Worksheet 13-1

30. Opinion.

31. Answers will vary (good—mother won't yell at you; bad—might have to wait longer before you can eat).

Worksheet 14-1

32. Opinion.

33. Answers will vary (I want to have a clean desk).

Worksheet 15-1

34. Opinion.

35. Answers will vary (I will follow all directions carefully when a project is assigned in art).

Worksheets 16-1 through 16-3

36. Opinion.

37. Answers will vary (recording number of minutes spent in an activity, number of days spent on an activity, how many times a behavior occurred in one day, etc.).

Worksheets 17-1 through 17-3

38. Opinion.

39. Opinion.

Worksheet 18-1

40. Opinion.

41. Answers will vary (so you don't lose sight of your original intent, so you can avoid the same mistakes later, etc.).

Worksheet 19-1

42. Opinion.

6. Inform students that they will have a test during the next class. They should take the responsibility for studying any worksheets with which they are unfamiliar and for asking questions before the test.

7. ASSIGNMENT: Assign students the task of studying the worksheets for a designated number of minutes, either at school if time is provided or at home. Ask students to record their starting and stopping times and the total number of minutes. The purpose of this is to provide the student with a structured study time and the responsibility of carrying through on a nonwritten assignment. Even if students protest that they know the material and do not need to study it, insist that they carry out the assignment because the extra practice will not hurt them.

8. Tell students to file all worksheets in their folders and to use the worksheets during their study time.

PROBLEM-SOLVING MODEL

Problem

What is a problem for you?

Behavior

What behavior is causing the problem or keeping it a problem?
Are you doing this behavior at the right time and place?

Choices

What other choices of behavior do you have in problem situations?

Consequences

What are the consequences (good/bad) of this behavior?
Would a different choice of behavior give a better consequence?

Goal

Why are you doing this behavior?
What do you really want to gain from this?
What goal would help you be a better student?

Plan

How are you going to change your behavior to reach your goal?

Keeping Track of Your Behavior

How are you going to keep track of your behavior and plan?
How long are you going to keep track of your behavior?

Reward

How will you reward yourself?
When will you reward yourself?
Is your reward realistic?

Evaluation

Did you use your plan?
Did you keep track of your behavior correctly?
Did you reach your goal?
Are you a better student?

REVIEW

Use this review guide to look over the material you have been given for Lessons 1 through 19. Make sure you know the answers to the questions. Put a checkmark in the box when you have studied each worksheet's material and know it thoroughly.

Worksheet 1-1 ☐
1. How does behavior affect your freedom?
2. What are some advantages to getting along well at school?

Worksheet 2-1 ☐
3. What are two kinds of students?
4. What are two characteristics of each kind of student?

Worksheet 3-1 and 3-2 ☐
5. What kind of student are you?
6. What is one area that you could improve in at school?
7. What is one area that you do well in at school?

Worksheet 4-1 ☐
8. Who is the person most responsible for making you a better student?
9. What is one of the most important ingredients for making your plan succeed?

Worksheet 5-1 ☐
10. Do you know the correct answers to any questions you missed on the quiz?

Worksheet 6-1 ☐
11. What are the responsibilities of the student in this contract?
12. What are the responsibilities of the teacher in this contract?
13. What reward was chosen?
14. What is the bonus reward?
15. What score (%) do you need for the bonus reward?

Worksheets 7-1 through 18-1 ☐
16. What do these symbols mean?

a.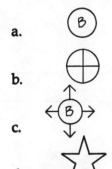

b.

c.

d.

e.

f.

g.

h.

17. Complete these review sentences:

    a. A behavior is something that you _____.

    b. Some behaviors usually happen at certain _____.

    c. Sometimes there is a _____ time or place for a behavior to happen.

    d. Most of the time, you can _____ what behavior you want to happen.

    e. A _____ is what happens because of a behavior.

    f. A behavior may have _____ than one consequence.

    g. Consequences of a behavior can be _____ or _____.

    h. Setting a goal means deciding what you _____.

    i. Your behavior helps you _____ your goal.

    j. Making a plan is deciding _____ you are going to reach your goal.

    k. You can tell if your plan is working by keeping _____ of your behavior.

    l. After you have done a good job on your plan, you can _____ yourself.

    m. You should evaluate your plan to see if it is making a _____ in your behavior.

Worksheet 7-1 ☐
18. Do you understand the material on this worksheet?
19. List three behaviors:

    a. _____

    b. _____

    c. _____

Worksheet 8-1 ☐
20. Do you understand the material on this worksheet?
21. List one behavior you would see at school but probably not at home.

Worksheet 9-1 ☐
22. Do you understand the material on this worksheet?
23. Why would it be difficult to do homework during a football game?

Worksheet 10-1 ☐
24. Do you understand the material on this worksheet?
25. What are two choices you would have if you fell down in the cafeteria?

    a. _____

    b. _____

Worksheet 11-1 ☐
26. Do you understand the material on this worksheet?
27. What might a consequence be for forgetting to brush your hair?

Worksheet 12-1 ☐

28. Do you understand the material on this worksheet?

29. What are two possible consequences of staying up all night watching TV the night before a big test?

a. _____

b. _____

Worksheet 13-1 ☐

30. Do you understand the material on this worksheet?

31. What is a good and a bad consequence for washing your hands before you eat dinner?

GOOD: _____

BAD: _____

Worksheet 14-1 ☐

32. Do you understand the material on this worksheet?

33. What is a possible goal for this behavior?

BEHAVIOR: I'm going to throw away all my old assignments and papers.

GOAL: _____

Worksheet 15-1 ☐

34. Do you understand the material on this worksheet?

35. What is a possible plan for this goal?

GOAL: I want to get an "A" on my art project.

PLAN: _____

Worksheets 16-1 through 16-3 ☐

36. Do you understand the material on this worksheet?

37. What are two ways to keep track of a behavior?

a. _____

b. _____

Worksheets 17-1 through 17-3 ☐

38. Do you understand the material on this worksheet?

39. What are two possible rewards for yourself?

a. _____

b. _____

Worksheet 18-1 ☐

40. Do you understand the material on this worksheet?

41. Why is it important to evaluate your plan?

Worksheet 19-1 ☐

42. Do you understand the material on this worksheet?

Lesson 20 TEST—DO YOU KNOW HOW TO BE A BETTER STUDENT?

Overview

The final lesson in Part One is a culmination of all major concepts presented in the previous lessons. If students have successfully reviewed the material, the test should present no surprises or problems for the students. The purpose of this lesson is to be an objective exercise for the students to demonstrate their knowledge of the material covered in the first part of this book. There are 43 items, worth a total of 55 points. An answer key and scoring percentages are provided. It is important to carry through on the contract (Lesson 6) that was intended to commit both parties (teacher and student) toward working on a common goal—that of successfully completing the workbook as indicated by the students' scores on the test.

Lesson Objective

- Students will score 90% or better on the test *or* will receive a score equal to or exceeding that determined to be the minimum acceptable score as previously stated by the teacher.

Teacher Preparation

Make enough copies of Worksheet 20-1, "Test," for your students. You may want to collate and assemble all pages of the test into one packet.

Lesson Plan

1. Ask students if they have any last-minute questions about the material previously covered.
2. Distribute the test packet, Worksheet 20-1.
3. Allow time for students to complete the test. Clarify items if necessary, but do not assist the students in any other way.
4. When students have completed the test, collect the tests for grading.
5. Review the questions and ask for student volunteers to supply answers. Correct responses as necessary. (The answer key is provided.)
6. Score tests according to the answer key. If you had determined that 90% was the mastery cutoff point, students would not be allowed to miss more than 5 points on the test.

7. Inform students of their scores.

8. Distribute or allow students to provide the predetermined reward according to the contract of Lesson 6.

9. If applicable, make plans to carry through on the bonus reward for the specified percentage on the test.

10. If applicable, inform students that they have done a very good job and are ready to continue with this project by beginning Part Two.

11. You may want to file the test in the students' folders.

Answer Key And Scoring

Points

(1)   1. Answers will vary. May include get better grades, stay out of trouble, learn to get along better with others when you have a job, and so on.

(2)   2. Good; could be better.

(2)   3. Answers will vary. May include (good) does his homework, turns in neat papers, and so on; (could be better) forgets assignments, is not prepared for class, and so on.

(1)   4. Answers will vary.

(1)   5. I am (myself).

(1)   6. Effort.

(1)   7. Contract.

(1)   8. Study the lessons, take a test.

(1)   9. Assist the student, encourage student, provide reward.

(1)   10. Answers will vary. Check contract.

(1)   11. Answers will vary. Check contract.

(1)   12. Behavior.

(1)   13. Do.

(2)   14. Answers will vary. May include studying, eating from a tray, looking up words in a dictionary, opening a locker, and so on.

(1)   15. Places.

(1)   16. Better (or best).

(3)   17. Answers will vary. May include (a) library, bedroom; (b) before class; (c) in the hallway, during lunch.

(1)   18. Choices.

(1)   19. Choose.

Points

(3)   20. Answers will vary. May include ignore him, hit him back, tell a teacher.

(1)   21. Consequence.

(1)   22. Consequence.

(1)   23. Answers will vary. May include get an "F" on the project, spend time after school doing it over or looking for it, and so on.

(1)   24. More than one consequence.

(1)   25. More.

(2)   26. Answers will vary. May include the teacher will send you back to your locker to get a pencil, you will have to borrow a pencil from someone else, you will miss test-taking time while you find another pencil, and so on.

(2)   27. Good, bad.

(2)   28. Answers will vary. May include (a) you will do better in English, (b) you will miss learning how to skate backward with your friends.

(1)   29. Goal.

(1)   30. Want.

(1)   31. Reach.

(1)   32. Answers will vary. May include to do a report for history on airplanes used in World War II.

(1)   33. Plan.

(1)   34. How.

(1)   35. Not sensible—it would take too long to finish the book.

(1)   36. Keeping track of a behavior.

(1)   37. Track.

(2)   38. Answers will vary. May include tally marks on a card, number of pages read, number of minutes spent studying, and so on.

(1)   39. Reward.

(1)   40. Reward.

(2)   41. Answers will vary. May include listening to the radio, buying oneself a food item or prize, going somewhere with a friend, not getting homework on Friday night, and so on.

(1)   42. Evaluation.

(1)   43. Difference (or change).

Scoring

No. points correct	%
55	100.0
54	98.2
53	96.1
52	94.5
51	92.7
50	90.1
49	89.1
48	87.2
47	85.5
46	83.6
45	81.8
44	80.0
43	78.2
42	76.4
41	74.5
40	72.7
39	70.9
38	69.1
37	67.3
36	65.5
35	63.6
34	61.8
33	60.0
32	58.2
31	56.4
30	54.5
29	52.7
28	50.9
27	49.1
26	47.3
25	45.5
24	43.6

No. points correct	%
23	41.8
22	40.0
21	38.2
20	36.4
19	34.5
18	32.7
17	30.9
16	29.1
15	27.3
14	25.5
13	23.6
12	21.8
11	20.0
10	18.2
9	16.4
8	14.5
7	12.7
6	10.9
5	9.1
4	7.3
3	5.5
2	3.6
1	1.8

Name _____ Date _____

Score _____

TEST

Points   *Lesson 1*

(1)   1. What is one advantage of getting along well in school?

_____

_____

Lesson 2

(2)   2. What are two types of students, as taught in this lesson?

a. _____

b. _____

(2)   3. List one characteristic of each type of student in part 2.

a. _____

b. _____

Lesson 3

(1)   4. What is one area that you could improve in at school?

_____

Lesson 4

(1)   5. Who is the person most responsible for helping you to become a better student?

_____

(1)   6. What is one of the most important ingredients for making your plan to be a better student succeed?

_____

Lesson 6

(1)   7. What document was completed and signed in this lesson?

_____

(1)   8. What is one responsibility of the student?

_____

(1)   9. What is one responsibility of the teacher?

_____

(1)   10. What reward was chosen?

_____

(1)   11. What score is necessary to receive a BONUS reward?

_____

Lesson 7

(1)   12. What does this symbol ⑧ stand for?

_____

(1)   13. A behavior is something that you _____ .

Lesson 8

(2)   14. List two behaviors that usually occur at school:

     a. _____

     b. _____

(1)   15. Some behaviors usually happen at certain _____ .

Lesson 9

(1)   16. Sometimes there is a _____ time or place for a behavior to occur.

(3)   17. What would be the best time or place for these behaviors to occur?

     a. Doing your homework: _____

     b. Asking about an assignment: _____

     c. Laughing with friends: _____

Lesson 10

(1)   18. What does this symbol ⊕ stand for?

_____

(1)   19. Most of the time, you can _____ what behavior you want to occur in a situation.

(3)   20. What are three alternative behaviors you could do in this situation: a kid knocks into you while you are walking down the hall.

     a. _____

     b. _____

     c. _____

Lesson 11

(1)   21. What does this symbol (β)→ stand for?

_____

(1)   22. A _____ is what happens because of a behavior.

(1)   23. What would most likely happen next in this situation: you forget to turn in your lab
project in science.

_____

_____

Lesson 12

(1)   24. What does this symbol ⬌Ⓑ⬍ stand for?

_____

(1)   25. A behavior may have _____ than one consequence.

(2)   26. List two consequences for this situation: you came to math class on the day of a test
without a pencil.

a. _____

b. _____

Lesson 13

(2)   27. Consequences of a behavior can be _____ or _____.

(2)   28. List two consequences of the following situation, related to the point of this lesson:
skipping roller skating with your friends to study English.

a. _____

b. _____

Lesson 14

(1)   29. What does this symbol ☆ stand for?

_____

(1)   30. Setting a goal means deciding what you _____.

(1)   31. Your behavior helps you _____ your goal.

(1)   32. What is a possible goal for the following behavior: you check out five books about
World War II from the library.

_____

_____

Lesson 15

(1)   33. What does this symbol 🪜 stand for?

_____

(1)   34. Making a plan is deciding _____ you are going to reach your goal.

(1)   35. What is wrong with this plan: my goal is to finish reading this book; my plan is to read one page a week.

_____

_____

Lesson 16

(1)   36. What does this symbol _____ stand for?

_____

(1)   37. You can tell if your plan is working by keeping _____ of your behavior.

(2)   38. List two ways to keep track of a behavior:

a. _____

b. _____

Lesson 17

(1)   39. What does this symbol _____ stand for?

_____

(1)   40. After you have done a good job on your plan, you can _____ yourself.

(2)   41. List two possible rewards for yourself:

a. _____

b. _____

Lesson 18

(1)   42. What does this symbol _____ stand for?

_____

_____

(1)   43. You should evaluate your plan to see if it is making a _____ in your behavior.

Total points possible: 55

Part Two

EXAMPLES OF HOW TO BE A BETTER STUDENT

Lesson 21 DO THESE STUDENTS LOOK FAMILIAR?

Overview

Now that students have completed Part One, they should be ready to put the bits of information together that they have learned and apply their knowledge to school settings and typical classroom-type problems. Part Two, "Examples of How to Be a Better Student," contains lessons that expose the student to cartoon characters with common school problems.

The first two lessons in each series discuss the basic problem of the student-model, the behavior involved, consequences of the behavior, behavioral choices/ alternatives, and possible goals and plans for the character to try. The students in the examples are fictitious, but their problems are not. Each problem is approached first in a very general way, considering several possible goals and plans before choosing a specific goal and plan.

The next three lessons in each series show the student-model in a school setting, encountering situations in which his or her plan can be utilized. The student goes through the situations with the model and has an opportunity to practice recording the behavior and examining the effectiveness of the plan. The model is not always 100% successful; often he or she "messes up" and tries again. Through the examples, there is opportunity to discuss the situation and offer suggestions for improving the plan.

The final two lessons in each series can be the most practical lessons for the students. These lessons assist the student in examining his or her own behavior, considering consequences and alternatives, and devising a plan to reach a goal. The student is given the option of using the plan presented by the model or creating his or her own. At the end of two weeks (or the duration of the "experiment"), the students are to present their projects to the class and to evaluate the effectiveness of them. Recounting their anecdotal experiences will also be of interest to the class. While some students are very adept at picking out other people's problems and what they should do to change, the key is really for the student to take an objective look at his or her own behavior deficits or excesses and become motivated to do something to change for the better.

Synopses of Student-Models and Strategies

Luther Lateagain has difficulty turning in his assignments on time. Although he generally completes the work eventually, he is usually late. Therefore, he stands a good chance of losing the assignment or getting a lower grade for not handing it in on time.

Luther's goal is to turn in 80% of his assignments on time, and his plan is to use an assignment chart to record the assignment and the due date and to indicate when he has finished the assignment and turned it in.

Holly Hoocares makes an attempt at doing her work, but she does not work carefully. Her work is usually characterized by careless mistakes, not following directions, and generally messy presentation.

Holly's goal is to improve her math grade to an 80% average on daily assignments. Her plan is to use a card that has cueing questions to ask herself before, during, and after working on the math assignment. She then is to record her daily math scores on an assignment sheet for a weekly average.

Dudley Dreamalot may sit in a classroom in body, but his thoughts are anywhere else but at school. Rather than pinpointing "daydreaming" as his main problem, a more general behavior of participating actively in class is selected.

Dudley's goal is to keep a checklist for his class that lists six participating behaviors and to participate in at least four of them daily. His plan is to review the checklist before, during, and after the class to remind himself to participate actively in that class.

In this introduction lesson to Part Two, students are given their first look at the three student-models with whom they will be "working" throughout the rest of Part Two. Based on the student-models' names, students are to make some preliminary judgments about the behaviors of these models.

Teacher Preparation

Make enough copies of Worksheet 21-1, "Does This Sound Familiar?" for your students.

Lesson Plan

1. Introduce this lesson by explaining that students will now be working with the information they have learned about choosing good behaviors by seeing how some other students handle their problems.

2. Distribute copies of Worksheet 21-1.

3. Ask for volunteers to read the comments at the top. Explain that in the next group of lessons, they will be meeting these student-models again. For now, though, the students are to think about their names and complete the rest of the worksheet by matching the comments to the student-model at the top who might have said each one.

4. Allow students time to complete the worksheet. Answers are

1. A		6. B	
2. B		7. B	
3. C		8. A	
4. A		9. C	
5. C		10. A	

5. REVIEW: (a) Ask students to summarize what they think Luther's, Holly's, and Dudley's main problems in school might be. (b) Tell students to file this worksheet in their folders.

6. ASSIGNMENT: Inform students that they will begin considering Luther Lateagain in detail in the next lesson. They should think about what problems might arise from late assignments.

DOES THIS SOUND FAMILIAR?

Here are three students who will become familiar to you. Look at their names and see if you can match the comments below to the right student.

A. Luther Lateagain   B. Holly Hoocares   C. Dudley Dreamalot

_____ 1. "Sorry that this assignment is late, teacher."

_____ 2. "This work was supposed to be done in pencil? Oh well . . . sorry."

_____ 3. "I can't wait to go fishing this weekend."

_____ 4. "I'll turn in that math paper tomorrow . . . maybe."

_____ 5. "I wonder what movie I'll go see tonight."

_____ 6. "So what if I forgot my name on my paper!"

_____ 7. "I don't know if the work is right, but I put down an answer for each problem."

_____ 8. "I don't have my homework from yesterday—but I found my science worksheet from two weeks ago. Here!"

_____ 9. "It sure was fun roller skating last week."

_____ 10. "I'll bring that project in tomorrow."

Lesson 22   LUTHER LATEAGAIN'S PROBLEM

Overview

In this lesson, students will meet the first student with a school problem: Luther Lateagain. Luther's main problem is that he doesn't turn in his assignments on time—and, in the meantime, the assignments get lost or destroyed and have to be redone to get credit.

Students should be given a five-page packet that includes an outline of the behavior, consequences, choices, goal, plan, record keeping, reward, and summary. Students will be given the correct answers for some of these sections; for others, they will choose logical responses and propose suggestions for Luther on their own. It would be most helpful for the students to keep this information together rather than as separate worksheets so that they can review what has already been established from day to day.

The complete program for Luther will probably take several days to complete. To keep the pace of the lessons going smoothly, you may want to vary the presentation of the material by having students work in small groups or in partners for some of the sections. Be sure to have the group come together at the end of each lesson, however, so that they can benefit from each other's ideas and hear the daily review.

Lesson Objectives

- Students will identify a hypothetical student's behavior problem.
- Students will identify at least two consequences of that behavior.
- Students will identify at least two behavioral choices that could be selected instead of the problem behavior.

Teacher Preparation

1. Make enough copies of Worksheet 22-1, "Meet Luther Lateagain," Worksheet 22-2, "Luther's Goal," Worksheet 22-3, "Luther's Plan," Worksheet 22-4, "Keeping Track of Those Assignments," and Worksheet 22-5, "Luther's Assignment Chart," for your students. Collate and staple the worksheets so that each student can be given an entire packet.
2. Copy the following on the chalkboard:

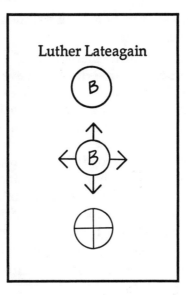

Lesson Plan

1. Introduce the lesson by stating that the class is now going to meet the first of several students who need some help to become better students. They are going to "assist" these students by going through the step-by-step procedure to figure out the problem and change the behavior.

2. Distribute the packet to students.

3. Instruct students to look at the first page (Worksheet 22-1) of the packet. Call on a volunteer to read Luther Lateagain's comments.

4. Direct the students' attention to the board. As you discuss the questions on the worksheet, refer to the symbols.

5. Direct students' attention to the "Behavior" section of the worksheet. Ask students to identify what behavior(s) is (are) preventing Luther from being a better student. Ideas may include forgetting about the assignment, losing the assignment, and turning the assignment in late.

6. Select "Turning in assignments late" as the behavior problem for Luther. You may want to write this on the board next to Ⓑ. Ask students for ideas as to why this may be a problem for Luther. (He's a procrastinator, is disorganized, may dislike a subject, etc.)

7. Direct students' attention to the "Consequences" section of the worksheet. Ask students to identify some consequences that may happen because Luther turns in assignments late. Ideas may include will have to redo the assignment, will lose the assignment, will have to miss something more enjoyable to look for the assignment, will get a lower grade

for turning in the assignment late. Ask students to consider whether any of the consequences sound good to them.

8. Direct students' attention to the "Choices" section of their worksheet. Explain to students that Luther does not have to turn in his assignments late; he chooses to. Students may argue that unfortunate events may have happened to Luther (for example, the dog ate his paper, he lost his book, he had to go to Boy Scouts), but ultimately it is Luther's responsibility to make sure that the assignment is correctly done and handed in *on time.* Ask students (either singly or in small groups) to think about other choices that Luther has involving turning in his assignments. Answers may include Luther could choose to do all of his assignments every day right after school, he could choose to ask the teacher for extra time on his assignments, he could choose to do all assignments for one class only.

9. Ask students to list at least two choices that Luther has. Have them put a star by the one they think is the best choice for Luther. (*Idea:* Pick one that mentions Luther's responsibility for turning in his assignments on time.)

10. REVIEW: (a) Ask students to summarize Luther's problem behavior, probable consequences, and a good choice for a better behavior. (b) Tell students to file this packet in their folders.

11. ASSIGNMENT: Inform students that the following day, they will continue to work on Luther's behavior. In the meantime, however, students should be aware of this behavior in their own experience. Inform them that in the next class, you will ask for examples of why their assignments are sometimes turned in late.

MEET LUTHER LATEAGAIN

Problem

Meet Luther Lateagain. Can you decide what he is having trouble with?

Behavior (B)

What behavior is stopping Luther from being a better student?

Consequences

What are some consequences of this behavior?

Choices

What other behavior choices does Luther have?

LUTHER'S GOAL

Goal

Choose one of the following goals for Luther to help him be a better student. Why did you pick that goal?

☐ **Goal A:**

I will turn in 100% of my assignments on time.

Only in my dreams!

☐ **Goal B:**

I will turn in 100% of my math assignments on time.

A+

☐ **Goal C:**

I will turn in 50% of my assignments on time.

The easy half!

☐ **Goal D:**

I will turn in 50% of my assignments within a week of their due date.

Getting closer!

☐ **Goal E:**

I will do all my assignments.

I'm wonderful!

☐ **Goal F:**

I will turn in 80% of my assignments on time.

My lucky number!

LUTHER'S PLAN

Plan

Luther has four plans to help him reach his goal. Which one do you think would help him the most?

☐ Plan A:

My mother will call the school every day to find out what my assignments are.

What's for science?

☐ Plan B:

My teacher will write down all my assignments in a notebook for me.

I have nothing better to do!

☐ Plan C:

I will do all my work with another student in my class so I will always know what to do.

Don't ever be absent!

☐ Plan D:

I will write down each assignment for each class every day on a chart and check it off when it is done and handed in.

We know...We know!

This sounds like work!

KEEPING TRACK OF THOSE ASSIGNMENTS

Keeping Track

What does Luther Lateagain need to know or do to get his assignments turned in on time? Put an X in front of each item that is important to help him be a better student.

_____ a. He needs to make an assignment sheet for each class.

_____ b. He needs to write each assignment on the sheet correctly.

_____ c. He needs to bring paper clips to class.

_____ d. He needs to know when each assignment is due.

_____ e. He needs to have someone tell him when the assignment is due.

_____ f. He needs to check off each assignment when it is done.

_____ g. He needs to have his mother check his work.

_____ h. He needs to know the weather report for Florida.

_____ i. He needs to hand in each assignment when it is done.

_____ j. He needs to have a digital watch with the date on it.

Reward ✳

Choose an appropriate reward for Luther. Write it on the line below.

When I reach my goal, I will
reward myself by _____
_____
_____.

Summary

Luther has a problem with _____.

He had decided to try to turn in _____ of his assignments on time.

His plan is to _____

_____.

Name _____ Date _____

LUTHER'S ASSIGNMENT CHART

Subject: _____ Week of : _____

DAY/DATE	ASSIGNMENT	DUE	DONE (✓)	HANDED IN (✓)
MONDAY				
TUESDAY				
WEDNESDAY				
THURSDAY				
FRIDAY				

This week I had _____ assignments to do.

I turned in _____ of them on time.

My percentage is _____%. Figure out percentage by using this formula:

$$\frac{\# \text{ of assignments done}}{\# \text{ of assignments due}} \times 100$$

Lesson 23 LUTHER'S GOAL AND PLAN

Overview

This lesson continues to examine Luther Lateagain's behavior in terms of devising a goal and plan. The student is given numerous choices from which to select, and he must justify why his choices are the best. Eventually the student will begin to formulate and carry out his own goals and plans for changing his behavior. This, and the following several examples, serves as practice for the student in making plausible, realistic decisions.

Lesson Objectives

- Students will choose an appropriate goal from several possible goals and explain why that goal is most appropriate for the given situation.
- Students will identify an appropriate plan from several possible plans and explain why it is the most appropriate for the given situation.

Teacher Preparation

Copies of Worksheets 22-2 and 22-3 should already be included in the packet of materials that was previously distributed to students.

Lesson Plan

1. Review material covered in the previous lesson by asking students to identify Luther Lateagain's behavior problem (turning in assignments late) and state at least one reason why this could be a problem (lower grades, redoing the assignments). Ask students to state what they concluded would be a better choice of behaviors for Luther (to turn in his assignments on time).

2. Ask students to locate the packet (Worksheets 22-1 through 22-5) from the previous day and to turn to Worksheet 22-2, "Luther's Goal."

3. Direct students' attention to the "Goal" section. Explain that several of the goals might be reasonable for Luther, but you want them to examine all of them and decide on the best goal for him. Discussion questions are

   Goal A
   a. Do you think this goal might be too hard for Luther? (it involves perfection, it might be too big a change to start with)
   b. How would Luther feel the first time he had a late assignment? (might give up because his goal has failed already)

c. Could he ever turn in a late assignment with this goal? (no, because there is no margin for error)

d. How do you feel about this goal? (answers will vary)

Goal B

a. Would this goal help Luther with his math assignments? (yes)

b. Would it help him with any of his other subjects? (no, not directly)

c. How do you feel about this goal for Luther? (answers will vary)

Goal C

a. Turning in half his assignments is better than none. Is 50% enough of a challenge? (probably not)

b. Do you think Luther should try harder than that? (yes)

c. How do you feel about this goal for Luther? (answers will vary)

Goal D

a. If Luther turns in his assignments a week after they are due, are they late or on time? (late)

b. Is this goal going to help him turn in his assignments on time? (no, it addresses a different problem)

c. How do you feel about this goal for Luther? (answers will vary)

Goal E

a. Even if Luther does the assignment, what is the other part of the problem? (turning it in, turning it in on time)

b. What happened to the math assignment that Luther did last week? (lost it)

c. Is doing an assignment the same behavior as turning it in? (no)

d. How do you feel about this goal for Luther? (answers will vary)

Goal F

a. Is 80% a reasonable amount to expect? (it's better than half)

b. Is Luther still going to have to put forth some effort to reach this goal? (yes)

c. How do you feel about this goal for Luther? (answers will vary, but this is probably the most reasonable)

d. If Luther turns in 78% of his assignments, has he reached this goal? (no, must be 80%)

e. If Luther turns in 92% of his assignments, has he reached his goal? (yes—and exceeded it)

Conclude that Goal F is probably the most reasonable goal for Luther in that it addresses the problem, requires effort, but not perfection, and would result in substantial improvement in Luther's behavior in this area.

4. Direct students' attention to the "Plan" section of Worksheet 22-3. Explain that now Luther knows where he's going, but he has to decide how he's going to get there. Call on volunteers to read each of the four plans highlighted on this worksheet and discuss each before coming up with the most appropriate plan or plans. (At this point, it may be helpful to indicate that several ideas can be incorporated into a plan; it does not have to be one single idea. On this worksheet, however, there is just one appropriate plan.) Discussion questions are

Plan A

a. Is it Luther's mother's behavior that needs to be addressed? (no)

b. Who needs to take responsibility of following a plan? (Luther)

Plan B

a. Is it Luther's teacher's behavior that needs to be addressed? (no)

b. Who needs to take responsibility of following a plan? (Luther)

Plan C

a. Who does Luther want to shift the responsibility to in this plan? (another student)

Plan D

a. How is Luther showing responsibility for following a plan in this situation? (writing down assignments, checking them off, not involving other people)

b. What do you think of this plan for Luther? (seems most appropriate)

5. REVIEW: (a) Ask students to summarize the best goal for Luther to help him be a better student about turning in his assignments on time. Why is this a reasonable goal? (b) Ask students to summarize a good plan for Luther. (c) Ask students to volunteer their own experiences with turning in assignments late—why this happens, what classes in particular are most difficult to keep track of assignments, what the teacher says that cues them to remember something about an assignment, and so on. (d) Tell students to file this packet of worksheets in their folders.

6. ASSIGNMENT: Inform students that on the next day, they will be helping Luther to keep track of his assignments. Ask them to bring in examples of how they presently keep track of their assignments for their classes.

Lesson 24   USING AN ASSIGNMENT CHART

Overview

This lesson concludes the analysis of how Luther could go about making a goal and devising a plan to reach the goal. Here, he specifically notes the tasks that must be considered for him to carry out his plan, chooses an appropriate reward, and designs an assignment chart to help him keep track of his assignments and their due dates.

Lesson Objectives

- Students will identify necessary subtasks for carrying out a specified plan for changing behavior.
- Students will identify an appropriate reward for reaching a goal.
- Students will demonstrate familiarity with a sample assignment chart by stating the various sections of it and their purpose.

Teacher Preparation

Copies of Worksheets 22-4 and 22-5 should already be included in the packet of materials that was previously distributed to students.

Lesson Plan

1. Review material previously discussed by asking students the following questions:

   What is Luther's basic problem? (turning in assignments on time)
   What is Luther's goal? (to turn in 80% of his assignments on time)
   What is Luther's plan? (to keep an assignment chart)

2. Ask students to locate the packet of Worksheets 22-1 through 22-5 from their folders and turn to Worksheet 22-4, "Keeping Track of Those Assignments."

3. Ask a student volunteer to read the "Keeping Track" section of the worksheet. Give students a few minutes to complete the task. Discuss the items. The answers are

   Luther will need to know or do items a, b, d, f, and i.

4. Ask students why they think it is important to keep track of the behavior they are working on changing. (It documents change in black and white, helps you to remember what you are looking for, creates an awareness of that behavior, etc.)

5. Direct students' attention to the "Reward" section of the worksheet. Have students complete the sentence by selecting an appropriate reward for Luther. Ideas may include going out for a pizza, buying a new record/tape, playing football with some friends, and so on. Any appropriate reward would be acceptable.

6. Direct students' attention to the "Summary" section and allow them a few minutes to complete the sentences. Answers are

> Luther has a problem with (turning in assignments on time).
>
> He has decided to try to turn in (80%) of his assignments on time.
>
> His plan is to (keep an assignment chart for his classes).

7. Direct students' attention to Worksheet 22-5, "Luther's Assignment Chart." Inform students that this is what Luther is going to use to help keep track of turning in his assignments.

8. Ask students if any of them has a system or technique that helps them keep track of their assignments. Allow time for sharing of ideas.

9. Discuss the various elements included on Luther's chart and try to compare the students' ideas with Luther's ideas. Ask students why this information may be important:

   a. *Subject*—so that all assignments for that class will be on the same page.
   b. *Week of*—so that students have a record of what was to be completed during any given week.
   c. *Day/Date*—a day-by-day record of each assignment.
   d. *Due*—the exact day/date that the assignment is to be finished.
   e. *Done*—the student's own monitoring of having completed the assignment as indicated by a checkmark.
   f. *Handed in*—the student's monitoring of having handed in a particular assignment.
   g. *Summary*—a method of calculating the percentage of turning in assignments for each class.

10. Inform students that during the next few lessons, they will be practicing filling out information for Luther on his assignment chart. Ask if there are any questions about what each section on the chart means or is for.

11. REVIEW: (a) Ask students to summarize why it is important to keep track of their assignments. (b) Ask students to mention specifically what information should be recorded on an assignment sheet. (c) Tell students to file this packet in their folders.

12. ASSIGNMENT: Inform students that on the next day, they will be practicing writing assignments. Ask them to be aware of how they use shortcuts to write down assignments for their various classes.

Lesson 25   PRACTICING LUTHER'S PLAN

Overview

In this lesson, students are given an opportunity to put Luther's plan into action by keeping track of fictitious assignments on his assignment chart. Thus, while students cannot actually follow Luther around and record his assignments, this activity can simulate Luther's behavior and activities by maintaining the assignment chart for him. Students will have the practice of filling out the sheet and translating oral assignments into written form. They will also encounter occasional setbacks by Luther to give students a chance to formulate ways to maintain accurate records even when things don't go perfectly according to plan. By convincing students that this is a simple, manageable way to keep track of assignments, you may find it is met with less resistance when the students themselves are required to keep their own records on their own assignments.

Lesson Objectives

- Students will accurately record oral assignments in written form on an assignment chart.
- Students will accurately record completed assignments and handed-in assignments on an assignment chart.

Teacher Preparation

1. Make enough copies of Worksheets 25-1, "Monday's Assignments," and Worksheet 25-2, "Tuesday's and Wednesday's Assignments," for your students.

2. Copy the following on the chalkboard:

Subject: _____		Week of: _____
DAY/DATE ASSIGNMENT DUE	DONE (✓)	HANDED IN (✓)

3. In this lesson, assignments are given to Luther for four different subjects—math, English, science, and social studies. There are several ways

this material can be used with your students. If desired, your entire class could concentrate on keeping track of assignments for only *one* of those subjects (especially if this task is new or confusing to your students); students may divide into four groups with each group being responsible for one of the four subjects, or the entire class may maintain four assignment charts for each of the four subjects. Depending on how you want to use the material, some thought needs to be given to how many assignment sheets need to be prepared for each of your students.

Lesson Plan

1. Introduce this lesson by reminding students that they will be filling out Luther's assignment sheet based on the information you will give them and that they will find on their worksheets. Ask students to locate Worksheet 22-5, "Luther's Assignment Chart," in their packet.

2. Discuss with students some shorthand notations used for recording assignments, such as "p" for "page"; "Soc. St.," for "social studies"; and so on.

3. Tell students which assignments they are to record if you do not want all students to record all four assignments. Make sure all students have the proper number of assignment charts, depending on how many subjects they are to record assignments for.

4. Distribute Worksheet 25-1, "Monday's Assignments," to students.

5. Demonstrate how the assignment for math class would be entered on the assignment chart by asking students to tell how it would be filled in. Write the students' responses on the board under the proper heading.

Subject: ___Math___	Week of: ___(current week)___			
DAY/DATE	ASSIGNMENT	DUE	DONE ($\checkmark$)	HANDED IN ($\checkmark$)
Monday	p. 115	Tuesday		

6. Allow students time to complete the assignment chart using the information on the remainder of the worksheet. The various assignment charts should resemble the following:

DAY/DATE	ASSIGNMENT	DUE
Monday	(English) write spelling words 17 times	Tuesday
Monday	(Science) bring 3 worms	Wednesday
Monday	(Soc. St.) color map of France	Friday

7. Ask students to listen carefully while you give them some more information about Luther's activities after he got home from school on Monday. They should record information on their practice sheets while you are reading the following:

> "Luther got home from school and decided to try to get some of that homework done right away. He did half his math problems, and then decided that division was taking too long so he would work on something else for awhile. He pulled out his spelling book and wrote each of the words 17 times. Then he went out in his backyard and dug up one earthworm and put it in the refrigerator in a little box. When his mother came home and opened the little box (looking for leftover chicken chow mein), she screamed and told Luther to go to his room. While in his room, Luther worked on coloring his map of France for awhile."

8. Allow students time to fill in the additional information on their assignment charts. The completed charts should now resemble the following:

DAY/DATE	ASSIGNMENT	DUE	DONE (✓)	HANDED IN (✓)
Monday	(Math) p. 115	Tuesday		
Monday	(English) write spelling words 17 times	Tuesday	✓	
Monday	(Science) bring 3 worms	Wednesday		
Monday	(Soc. St.) color map of France	Friday		

9. Summarize the information so far by asking the following questions for each subject:

   a. How many assignments has Luther completed now?

   b. How many assignments has he handed in?

   c. How many assignments does he have yet to complete?

   d. Are any assignments late?

10. Explain that in Luther's life it is now Tuesday morning. As you read the synopsis of what happened before he went to school on Tuesday, students should update their assignment charts for Luther, listening for the pertinent information they need to record. Read the following to the students:

    "Luther's dog got into his room (searching for homework to chew on, no doubt) and woke Luther up. Luther decided to get up and try to finish some homework before school. He sat at his desk and finished the rest of his math assignment. It didn't take him as long as he thought it would, so he went outside and dug up two more earthworms before breakfast. Then he had a big breakfast of eggs and sausages and went to school. Luther got to school on time and gave his math teacher the math assignment. Then he went to the science lab and gave his earthworms to his science teacher. But somehow, somewhere, he could not find his spelling assignment. He cleaned out his books, his locker, and even checked his socks, but that assignment was nowhere to be found."

11. Allow students time to complete the assignment sheet. Answer questions about Luther's activities if students missed some information.

12. Ask students to summarize their information so far by answering the following questions for each subject:

    a. How many assignments did Luther complete now?
    b. How many assignments have been handed in?
    c. How many assignments does Luther need to finish?
    d. Are any assignments late?

13. Direct students' attention to Worksheet 25-2, "Tuesday's and Wednesday's Assignments." Instruct students to record the pertinent information from the class assignments for Tuesday on their assignment charts. Completed charts should resemble the following:

DAY/DATE	ASSIGNMENT	DUE	DONE (✓)	HANDED IN (✓)
Tuesday	(Math) p. 116	Thursday		
Tuesday	(Eng.) sentences	Wednesday		
Tuesday	(Science) Part C	Friday		
Tuesday	(Soc. St.) p. 150 (1–10)	Wednesday		

14. Have the students listen while you read the following paragraph about Luther's activities after school on Tuesday evening. They should record information while listening.

    "Luther finished his spelling sentences during class time and handed them in right away. He didn't want to have to make up *two* English assignments! After school, after watching television for three hours, he worked for a little while on the map of France until his blue marker wore out. He decided to work on some of page 116 in math until he fell asleep."

15. Summarize the information so far by asking the following questions for each subject:

    a. How many assignments are done now?

    b. How many assignments have been handed in this week?

    c. How many does Luther have left to do?

    d. How many are late?

16. Have students listen while you read the following paragraph about Luther's morning on Wednesday. They should record the necessary information on the assignment sheet.

    "Wednesday morning, Luther woke up early and felt very good. He finished the rest of page 116 in his math book and did the social studies assignment on page 150. Wednesday at school, Luther handed in his math assignment, but he couldn't find his social studies assignment. His teacher told him that he would still get partial credit if it was turned in on Thursday."

17. Allow time for students to ask questions about any missing information or recording problems on the assignment sheet.

18. Direct students' attention to "Wednesday's Assignments" on the lower half of Worksheet 25-2. Allow students time to record pertinent information from this worksheet on the assignment chart for Luther.

19. Have the students listen while you read the following paragraph about Wednesday's activities after school. Students should be recording information on the assignment sheet.

    "Wednesday after school, Luther finished coloring the map of France and put it carefully in his social studies book so he wouldn't lose it. Since his book was open now anyway, he went ahead and did the questions on page 151. Then he did half his math on page 117 and began working on his spelling story."

20. Summarize the information so far by asking the following questions for each subject:

    a. How many assignments are done now?

    b. How many have been handed in?

    c. How many does Luther have left to do?

    d. Are any assignments late?

21. Allow students time to ask questions about the assignments or discuss any problems in filling out the charts they have encountered. Compare

students' answers with the completed assignment charts at the end of this lesson.

22. REVIEW: (a) Ask students to summarize today's activities, stating specifically what they found difficult about the recordkeeping activity and what benefits they think are likely to happen by doing this activity. (b) Tell students to file the worksheets in their folders. (c) Inform students that the next lesson will complete the rest of Luther's assignments for the week and that they will find out if Luther met his goal or not.

MONDAY'S ASSIGNMENTS

Use Luther's assignment chart to help him record the missing information.

Math class:

English class:

Science class:

Social studies class:

TUESDAY'S AND WEDNESDAY'S ASSIGNMENTS

Use Luther's assignment chart to help him record the missing information.

Tuesday's Assignments

Math class:

> Do the problems on page 116 by Thursday.

English class:

> Write a sentence using each spelling word at least once by tomorrow. You will have time to get started in class.

Science class:

> Do Part C in your lab workbook for Friday.

Social studies class:

> Answer questions 1 through 10 on page 150 for tomorrow.

Wednesday's Assignments

Math class:

> You all need much more practice on long division. Do page 117 for tomorrow.

English class:

> I would like for you to write an incredibly, wonderful creative story for me by Friday.

Science class:

> Guess what, class? We're having a movie today! No written assignment!!

Social studies class:

> Please do the questions on page 151. Turn them in tomorrow. Don't forget your map by Friday.

LUTHER'S ASSIGNMENT CHART

Subject: __Math__   Week of: __4/14__

DAY/DATE	ASSIGNMENT	DUE	DONE (✓)	HANDED IN (✓)
MONDAY	p. 115	Tues.	✓	✓
TUESDAY	p. 116	Thurs.	✓	✓
WEDNESDAY	p. 117	Thurs.		
THURSDAY				
FRIDAY				

This week I had _____ assignments to do.

I turned in _____ of them on time.

My percentage is _____%. Figure out percentage by using this formula:

$$\frac{\text{\# of assignments done}}{\text{\# of assignments due}} \times 100$$

LUTHER'S ASSIGNMENT CHART

Subject: **English**   Week of : **4/14**

DAY/DATE	ASSIGNMENT	DUE	DONE (✓)	HANDED IN (✓)
MONDAY	Write spell. words 17x	Tues.	✓	lost
TUESDAY	Sentences	Wed.	✓	✓
WEDNESDAY	Write a story	Fri.		
THURSDAY				
FRIDAY				

This week I had _____ assignments to do.

I turned in _____ of them on time.

My percentage is _____%. Figure out percentage by using this formula:

$$\frac{\text{\# of assignments done}}{\text{\# of assignments due}} \times 100$$

LUTHER'S ASSIGNMENT CHART

Subject: __Science_____ Week of: __4/14_____

DAY/DATE	ASSIGNMENT	DUE	DONE (✓)	HANDED IN (✓)
MONDAY	Bring 3 worms	Wed.	✓	✓
TUESDAY	Part C	Fri.		
WEDNESDAY	No assign.			
THURSDAY				
FRIDAY				

This week I had _____ assignments to do.

I turned in _____ of them on time.

My percentage is _____%. Figure out percentage by using this formula:

$$\frac{\text{\# of assignments done}}{\text{\# of assignments due}} \times 100$$

LUTHER'S ASSIGNMENT CHART

Subject: __Social Studies__   Week of: __4/14__

DAY/DATE	ASSIGNMENT	DUE	DONE (✓)	HANDED IN (✓)
MONDAY	Color map of France	Fri.	✓	
TUESDAY	p. 150 (1-10)	Wed.	✓	lost
WEDNESDAY	Ques. on p. 151	Thurs.	✓	
THURSDAY				
FRIDAY				

This week I had _____ assignments to do.

I turned in _____ of them on time.

My percentage is _____%. Figure out percentage by using this formula:

$$\frac{\text{\# of assignments done}}{\text{\# of assignments due}} \times 100$$

Lesson 26   HOW DID LUTHER DO?

Overview

In this lesson, the students will receive their final practice session on recording assignments for Luther. Following this, they have an evaluation form to consider and fill out. They will calculate the number of assignments completed and handed in on time to determine whether or not Luther reached his goal. They are also given an opportunity to express their opinions about this plan for Luther and for themselves.

Lesson Objectives

- Students will accurately record assignments and progress toward completing them and handing them in.
- Students will evaluate this plan for Luther by determining its workability and success in the hypothetical case studied.

Teacher Preparation

1. Make enough copies of Worksheet 26-1, "Thursday's Assignments," and Worksheet 26-2, "Evaluation Form: How Did Luther Do?," for your students.
2. Copy the column headings from Luther's assignment chart on the chalkboard if you found this helpful for your students.

Subject: _____		Week of: _____		
DAY/DATE	ASSIGNMENT	DUE	DONE ( )	HANDED IN ( )

Lesson Plan

1. Ask students to locate Worksheet 22-5 to continue recording Luther's assignments. Again, if students are recording more than one subject's assignments, they should have one copy of the assignment chart for each subject.

2. Explain that today they will continue and finish the practice exercises on filling out Luther's assignment sheet and will then evaluate how well his plan worked.

3. Explain that it is now Thursday morning in Luther's life. As you read the following summary of Luther's events, students should listen and update their assignment sheets for Luther.

> "Thursday morning, Luther overslept and didn't have time to work on any homework that morning. He ran through the kitchen and almost out of the house before he remembered to get the homework that he had finished the night before. Jumping over his dog (who was afraid of getting blamed for not waking up Luther), he grabbed his social studies book as he ran to school. After arriving at school, he dashed over to his social studies teacher and threw the questions he had answered and the map of France (neatly colored, of course) on the teacher's desk. 'Did you notice, it's handed in *early?*' asked Luther. He went on to his math class, ready to start the day."

4. Allow students time to complete the assignment sheet and answer any questions they may have.

5. Distribute Worksheet 26-1 to students.

6. Call on volunteers to read the instructions. Allow time for students to complete the assignment sheet with the information from the worksheet.

7. Direct students' attention to the assignment sheet. Explain that you are going to read about Luther's day at school on Thursday. They should be listening for information to complete the assignment chart.

> "Thursday, during science study hall, Luther managed to finish his science assignment (Part C), and he handed it in right away. He also had time to finish his two math assignments, pages 117 and 118. It turned out that division was not as bad as he had thought! After school, Luther went home, turned on the television, turned off the television, and did not come out of his room until he had written each of his spelling words for the week 17 times. He didn't know if his English teacher had forgotten about it by now or not, but he decided to hope for the best. Luther also did his social studies assignment (page 152), wrote a fast (but very entertaining) story for English, and found his social studies paper (page 150) under the bed along with his dirty socks for the week. After spraying the room and the social studies paper, he finished his English (page 100). Then he ate supper, watched television, and went to bed."

8. Ask students to summarize their assignment charts so far by asking the following questions about each subject:

  a. How many assignments are done now?

  b. How many assignments have been handed in?

  c. How many assignments are left for Luther to do?

  d. Are any assignments still late?

9. Answer any questions about filling in the charts that the students may have.

10. Have students listen as you read the final paragraph about Luther's activities on Friday morning.

   "Friday morning, Luther got up early, fed the dog, put on clean socks, ate a nutritious breakfast, and carefully collected all his books and assignments before heading off to school. At school, Luther first went to math class and handed in pages 117 and 118. Then he went to English and turned in his story. 'I'm sure they'll want to make a movie of it,' he winked to his surprised teacher. He also handed in his assignment from page 100 and the spelling words neatly written 17 times. 'Why, Luther,' exclaimed his English teacher, 'I'd forgotten all about that assignment.' Then she winked. In science, Luther asked Mr. Boom how the earthworms were doing while the other students were handing in Part C. After that, he went to social studies and deposited page 150 (late, but better late than never) and page 152 on the teacher's desk. Then he breathed a sigh of relief and made plans to go to the basketball game that night with some friends (since he didn't have to worry about doing any homework!)."

11. Allow students time to complete the assignment sheet with the information and answer any questions they may have.

12. Compare students' answers with the completed assignment charts at the end of this lesson.

13. Distribute Worksheet 26-2, "Evaluation Form: How Did Luther Do?," to students. If students only completed a portion of the project, they should complete only the questions about the assignments they did. Information for part 5 is a compilation of all four subjects. If students were divided into groups, this should be compiled as a class project to determine whether or not Luther reached his goal. Here are the answers:

1. a. 4;   b. 3;   c. 75%;   d. no
2. a. 4;   b. 3;   c. 75%;   d. no
3. a. 2;   b. 2;   c. 100%;   d. yes
4. a. 4;   b. 3;   c. 75%;   d. no
5. a. 14;   b. 11;   c. 79%;   d. no;   e. opinion;   f. opinion

14. REVIEW: (a) Have students offer their opinions as to Luther's goal, plan, and behavior change. What elements did they find easy to deal with? What was difficult? Was the goal a good one? Was the plan effective? If not, why not? Do they suspect that if Luther continued the plan for a second week, he would reach his goal of 80%? (b) Explain to students that in the next class meeting, they will begin working on keeping track of their own assignments, much as Luther did. They should be thinking about any changes in the assignment chart they would like to include, if any. (c) Tell students to file their worksheets in their folders.

THURSDAY'S ASSIGNMENTS

Use Luther's assignment chart to help him record the missing information.

Math class:

Now we're going to learn long division with remainders. What fun! Do page 118 by Friday.

English class:

You're getting a test tomorrow. Answer the review questions on page 100.

Science class:

YAY!!!

Mr. Boom is not here today. He is babysitting with some ill earthworms at home. We shall use today's science class for a QUIET study hall.

Social studies class:

I would like you to write out the vocabulary words on page 152, 1 through 20, in your book for tomorrow. Don't forget about that map of France, due tomorrow!

The map is DONE, DONE, DONE!!!

EVALUATION FORM: HOW DID LUTHER DO?

Use Luther's assignment charts to complete this evaluation.

1. MATH

____ a. How many assignments did Luther have to do for math?

____ b. How many did he turn in on time?

____ c. What percentage of assignments did he turn in on time?

____ d. Did Luther reach his goal of turning in 80%?

2. ENGLISH

____ a. How many assignments did Luther have to do for English?

____ b. How many did he turn in on time?

____ c. What percentage of assignments did he turn in on time?

____ d. Did Luther reach his goal of turning in 80%?

3. SCIENCE

____ a. How many assignments did Luther have to do for science?

____ b. How many did he turn in on time?

____ c. What percentage of assignments did he turn in on time?

____ d. Did Luther reach his goal of turning in 80%?

4. SOCIAL STUDIES

____ a. How many assignments did Luther have to do for social studies?

____ b. How many did he turn in on time?

____ c. What percentage of assignments did he turn in on time?

____ d. Did Luther reach his goal of turning in 80%?

5. ALL ASSIGNMENTS

____ a. How many assignments did Luther have to do for all four classes?

____ b. How many assignments did he turn in on time?

____ c. What percentage of assignments did he turn in on time?

____ d. Did Luther reach his goal of turning in 80%?

____ e. Do you think Luther should try this plan again for another week?

____ f. Should he change anything? What? _____

LUTHER'S ASSIGNMENT CHART

Subject: __Math__   Week of : __4/14__

DAY/DATE	ASSIGNMENT	DUE	DONE (✓)	HANDED IN (✓)
MONDAY	p. 115	Tues.	✓	✓
TUESDAY	p. 116	Thurs.	✓	✓
WEDNESDAY	p. 117	Thurs.	✓	✓ Late
THURSDAY	p. 118	Fri.	✓	✓
FRIDAY				

This week I had _____4_____ assignments to do.

I turned in _____3_____ of them on time.

My percentage is _____75_____%. Figure out percentage by using this formula:

$$\frac{\text{\# of assignments done}}{\text{\# of assignments due}} \times 100$$

LUTHER'S ASSIGNMENT CHART

Subject: **English**   Week of: **4/14**

DAY/DATE	ASSIGNMENT	DUE	DONE (✓)	HANDED IN (✓)
MONDAY	Write spell. words 17x	Tues.	✗ ✓	Lost ✓ Late
TUESDAY	Sentences	Wed.	✓	✓
WEDNESDAY	Write a story	Fri.	✓	✓
THURSDAY	p.100 questions Test- Friday	Fri.	✓	✓
FRIDAY				

This week I had **4** assignments to do.

I turned in **3** of them on time.

My percentage is **75** %. Figure out percentage by using this formula:

$$\frac{\text{\# of assignments done}}{\text{\# of assignments due}} \times 100$$

LUTHER'S ASSIGNMENT CHART

Subject: __Science__   Week of: __4/14__

DAY/DATE	ASSIGNMENT	DUE	DONE (✓)	HANDED IN (✓)
MONDAY	Bring 3 worms	Wed.	✓	✓
TUESDAY	Part C	Fri.	✓	✓
WEDNESDAY	No assign.			
THURSDAY	No assign.			
FRIDAY				

This week I had _____2_____ assignments to do.

I turned in _____2_____ of them on time.

My percentage is _____100_____ %. Figure out percentage by using this formula:

$$\frac{\text{\# of assignments done}}{\text{\# of assignments due}} \times 100$$

LUTHER'S ASSIGNMENT CHART

Subject: __Social Studies__   Week of: __4/14__

DAY/DATE	ASSIGNMENT	DUE	DONE (✓)	HANDED IN (✓)
MONDAY	Color map of France	Fri.	✓	✓
TUESDAY	p. 150 (1-10)	Wed.	✗ ✓	lost late
WEDNESDAY	Ques. on p. 151	Thurs.	✓	✓
THURSDAY	Vocab. words p. 152 (1-20)	Fri.	✓	✓
FRIDAY				

This week I had _____4_____ assignments to do.

I turned in _____3_____ of them on time.

My percentage is _____75_____%. Figure out percentage by using this formula:

$$\frac{\text{\# of assignments done}}{\text{\# of assignments due}} \times 100$$

Lesson 27 APPLICATION—DON'T BE A LUTHER LATEAGAIN

Overview

If students have successfully learned and applied their learning from the previous lessons to Luther Lateagain and his situation, they should now be ready to make the transition to using these techniques to cope with their own school situation. Keeping track of assignments and turning them in on time is a very basic school skill. While some students may insist that they can remember everything without writing it down, it is still good practice for them to learn techniques for being systematic in recording information, observing events accurately, and evaluating themselves. Goal setting and self-monitoring are skills that encompass a wide variety of school and life situations. Teacher considerations for this final lesson on turning in assignments on time include

1. Do you want all students to use the same recording form or will you allow for individual forms?
2. Do you want students to record all assignments or focus on one or two subjects at this time?
3. Do you want to continue this project for a week, two weeks, or other amount of time?

Once you have decided on the parameters of this assignment, based on your own situation, the rest of the project can be carried out. Class time, especially at the beginning of this project, will need to be devoted to working out individual problems. As students begin to work through these problems and develop a system they can live with, less time will need to be given to problem solving and more time can be spent on evaluating and simply checking up on the assignment sheet.

As problems arise, you should allow class time for students to talk about what others might do to resolve the difficulty. Minor modifications can be made in the plan throughout the project, but basic goals should remain the same throughout so that students have the experience of setting realistic goals.

This entire project can be a graded, required assignment for students. Whether or not you wish to have the students continue using an assignment sheet following the project is optional. It is hoped that the students will have come to see the value of carrying out such a project and will transfer these skills to school situations for their *own* benefit.

Lesson Objectives

- Students will devise a plan for improving their school skill of turning in assignments on time.

- Students will set and reach a realistic goal for the school skill of turning in assignments on time.
- Students will accurately record their behavior for the school skill of turning in assignments on time.

Teacher Preparation

1. Make enough copies of Worksheet 27-1 (two pages), "Student Worksheet," for your students.

2. You may want to copy the following symbols on the chalkboard to refer to as the different sections are discussed on the worksheet.

3. You may want to make copies of the sample assignment chart in Worksheet 27-2 for your students to use if they will not be developing their own.

Lesson Plan

1. Inform students that they are now ready to leave Luther Lateagain and work on their own situations. Remind them that they should use the things they learned from working out Luther's problems to solve their own school problems. Explain that this lesson will help them with that.

2. Distribute Worksheet 27-1 (two pages) to students.

3. Discuss questions on the worksheet and allow students time to record their opinions and/or commitments to making a plan and goal.

    a. Question 5: Have students discuss the usual consequences for not turning in assignments on time. This may vary from teacher to teacher or class to class.

    b. Question 6: Remind students that they have alternative choices as far as their behavior is concerned. If they are not satisfied with their behavior in this area, this is a time of evaluation for them to decide on a better behavioral choice.

    c. Question 8: Make sure that students decide on a number or percentage in writing their goal. This will make it much easier to measure at the end when they evaluate their plan and goal.

d. Question 9: For the sake of convenience, have students try to stay within a two-week time frame for reaching their goal.

e. Question 10: This is a question of commitment, asking the student to reiterate what behavior it is that he or she is going to change. It might be *doing* the assignment (if that is the major problem), turning it in, turning it in on time, and so on. The intent here clearly is to drive home to the student what it is that needs to be changed. Monitoring the behavior alone is not likely to change anything if he or she only monitors how many assignments are late; changing the behavior is what will make a difference.

f. Question 11: Students may want to brainstorm to give each other ideas for their plans.

g. Question 12: Students must decide on a plan of action.

h. Question 13: Students are to list the things that need to be done before the plan can be carried out. This may include running off copies of an assignment chart, cleaning up the desk or work area to make a space for keeping finished assignments, getting a small notebook, and so on.

i. Question 15: This is a summary statement to help students keep their goal in mind. An example might read, "At the end of *two weeks,* I will look at my *assignment notebook* and see whether or not I have *turned in more math assignments on time.* If my percentage is 75% or higher, I have reached my goal."

j. Question 16: Students select an appropriate reward for themselves, subject to the teacher's approval and discretion. You may want to offer the students some classroom privileges (a party, a movie).

4. Allow time for any specific questions, comments, or problems with the worksheet and development of their plans and goals.

5. Tell students to file their worksheets in their folders.

6. Decide when your class will begin the actual carrying out of their projects. You may want to give them a day or two to acquire all needed materials and to make sure they each have some sort of workable assignment sheet or recording plan.

7. For the next week or however long you have determined that this project will be continued, class time should be set aside for monitoring the class' participation and having brief discussions on the problems and/or successes that they are experiencing. A more thorough evaluation will be conducted at the end of the class project. Keep in mind the following:

a. Some students will find it difficult to get started and to keep up with this project. Remind them that this is an assignment and you expect them to complete all of the information. Keep after them!

b. When you have your class discussions on the project, ask for examples of how it is helping them keep track of their assignments. Students can be great motivators of each other.

c. Have students share ideas with each other. It may be far more meaningful for a student to adapt an idea from another student than merely to follow the teacher's commands.

d. Praise students often for keeping up with their assignments and recording the information correctly.

STUDENT WORKSHEET

1. *Behavior:* Is this behavior, turning in assignments on time, something that would help make you a better student?

   (B) _____

2. Do you do your assignments? _____

3. Do you remember to turn them in on time? _____

4. Are there any classes in particular that you have trouble with?_____

5. *Consequences:* What are the consequences when you don't turn in your assignments on time?

   (B) _____
   _____
   _____

6. *Choices:* What choices do you have regarding turning in your assignments on time?_____

   ⊕ _____
   _____

7. What is the best choice for you? _____
   _____

8. *Goal:* What goal will you set for yourself?

   ☆ My goal is to: _____

9. How long do you think it will take you to reach your goal? _____
   _____

10. How are you going to change your behavior to reach your goal? _____
    _____

11. *Plan:* What are some ideas for your plan to reach your goal?

    I could _____
    I could _____
    I could _____

12. Choose a plan. I pick: _____

13. What do you need to do or get to carry out the plan?

_____

_____

_____

14. How will you keep track of your behavior and plan? (You can use a chart like Luther's or you might want to make up your own.)

15. How will you know you have reached your goal?

At the end of _____, I will look at my _____
                (how long?)   (chart?)

and see whether or not I have _____ .
                          (what behavior are you changing?)

If my percentage is _____ or higher, I have reached my goal.
                  (what percentage?)

16. *Reward:*   How will you reward yourself? _____

          When will you reward yourself? _____

GOOD LUCK!

We will evaluate your plan and goal on _____ .
                                    (date)

Name _____ Date _____

SAMPLE ASSIGNMENT CHART

Subject: _____ Week of : _____

DAY/DATE	ASSIGNMENT	DUE	DONE (✓)	HANDED IN (✓)
MONDAY				
TUESDAY				
WEDNESDAY				
THURSDAY				
FRIDAY				

This week I had _____ assignments to do.

I turned in _____ of them on time.

My percentage is _____%. Figure out percentage by using this formula:

$$\frac{\text{\# of assignments done}}{\text{\# of assignments due}} \times 100$$

Lesson 28 EVALUATION OF YOUR PROJECT

Overview

After the students have conducted their project for whatever length of time was decided upon (one or two weeks), they should reassemble to discuss their projects, problems, successes, and observations. The purpose of this final evaluation is to learn from each other and to propose ideas for improving their plans if this project is to be continued. Most important, students should have experienced some success in managing their own behavior and be on the road to making further improvements in their school skills.

Lesson Objectives

- Students will determine whether or not they have reached their goal.
- Students will specify modifications for their plan to improve it if it were to be continued.

Teacher Preparation

Make enough copies of Worksheet 28, "Evaluation Questions," for your students.

Lesson Plan

1. Have students assemble all paperwork that was used in carrying out their project (for example, assignment sheets).
2. Distribute Worksheet 28-1 to students.
3. Inform students that now that they have worked on their projects for awhile, they are ready to determine whether or not they have reached the goal they set for themselves.
4. Discuss the questions on the worksheet. You may call on volunteers to explain their plans and give more detailed accounts of what worked or did not work for them. Make sure that students record their answers on the evaluation sheet.
5. Conclude the discussion by asking students if they thought this was a helpful project for them. Inform them that they will be learning other helpful techniques in future lessons.
6. Tell students to file their worksheets and other paperwork in their folders.
7. You may want to give each student a grade on their project. This grade could be based on effort, thoroughness of the plan, appropriateness of the goal, and/or behavioral change.

EVALUATION QUESTIONS

1. What was your goal? ————————————————————————————————

2. What was your plan? ————————————————————————————————

3. How long did you try your plan? ———————————————————————

4. Did you use the example plan or develop your own? ——————————

5. Describe your plan (what did you do to carry out the plan, how did you keep track of your behavior, how did you reward yourself?)

   ——

   ——

   ——

   ——

6. Did your plan work for you? ——————————————————————————

7. Did you reach your goal? ————————————————————————————

8. What problems did you have with your plan? ——————————————

   ——

   ——

9. What worked well about your plan? ————————————————————

   ——

   ——

10. What would you change or keep if you continued this project? ————

    ——

11. What ideas do other people have about your plan? ————————————

    ——

12. What other plans did people have for the same problem? ——————

    ——

13. Is this still a problem for you? If so, can you think of another plan? ——

    ——

Lesson 29 HOLLY HOOCARES' PROBLEM

Overview

Students are introduced to Holly Hoocares, a girl whose main problem is turning in careless work. It appears that Holly will give a halfhearted effort toward doing her assignments, but doesn't like to take the time to make sure she understands the directions, doesn't follow the directions consistently and accurately, and doesn't proofread the final product before handing it in.

Students should be given a five-page packet that includes Holly's problem behavior, questions about consequences and choices, and possible goals, plans, and recordkeeping activities for Holly.

The format for the next few lessons is essentially the same as that of Luther Lateagain's. Again, it is most helpful if information is reviewed daily and as a class project so that students can benefit from each other's comments and observations.

Holly selects math assignments as the target for recording her changed behavior; however, suggestions and ideas are given in Lesson 33 for adapting the techniques to other subjects.

Lesson Objectives

- Students will identify a hypothetical student's behavior problem.
- Students will identify at least two consequences of that behavior.
- Students will identify at least two behavioral choices that could be selected instead of the problem behavior.

Teacher Preparation

1. Make enough copies of Worksheets 29-1 through 29-5 for your students. These pages can be collated and stapled so that they can be given to each student as an entire packet.
2. Copy the following on the chalkboard:

Lesson Plan

1. Introduce the lesson by stating that the next problem they are going to consider belongs to a girl named Holly Hoocares. As they may have guessed from her name, she is fairly apathetic about her schoolwork. Their job is to help Holly overcome this problem and be a better student.

2. Distribute the packet to students.

3. Instruct students to look at the first page of the packet, which is Worksheet 29-1, "Meet Holly Hoocares." Call on a volunteer to read Holly's comments.

4. Direct students' attention to the board. As you discuss the questions on the worksheet, refer to the symbols.

5. Direct students' attention to the "Behavior" section of the worksheet. Ask students to identify what behavior is preventing Holly from being a better student. Ideas may include not following directions, forgetting to look at the sign in front of the problems, or working too quickly.

6. Summarize students' responses by selecting "doing careful work" as the desired behavior and "doing careless" work as the problem. You may want to write this on the board next to ⓑ.

7. Direct students' attention to the "Consequences" section of the worksheet. Ask students to think of some consequences that may happen because of Holly's careless work. Ideas may include

   Holly will get a bad grade on her assignment because of careless mistakes, a messy paper, or not following the directions.

   Holly will memorize mistakes, thinking that she had copied or done the work correctly.

Holly's teacher will think that Holly really doesn't know how to do the work.

Ask students to consider whether any of the consequences are good ones.

8. Direct students' attention to the "Choices" section of their worksheet. Explain that Holly does not have to turn in sloppy or careless work; she chooses to. Allow students time to think about why Holly might choose to do this; perhaps she would rather finish her work in a hurry to allow time to do something fun; perhaps she doesn't particularly like a subject; or perhaps she doesn't understand what to do and is afraid to ask. Still, Holly is choosing to allow this behavior to happen instead of making an effort to change things. Ask students to consider other choices for Holly. Ideas may include

> Holly could choose to proofread her assignments.
>
> Holly could choose to get a tutor for subjects that she has trouble with.
>
> Holly could choose to try to improve her grades in her worst subject.
>
> Holly could choose to get extra help from the teacher when she doesn't understand something.
>
> Holly could choose to work slowly on assignments instead of racing through them.

9. On their worksheet, ask students to list at least two choices that Holly has regarding improving her behavior. Have them put a star by the one they think is the best choice for Holly. (Idea: Pick one that mentioned Holly's responsibility for doing quality work.)

10. REVIEW: (a) Ask students to summarize Holly's problem behavior, probable consequences, and a good choice for a better behavior. (b) Tell students to file this packet in their folders.

11. ASSIGNMENT: Inform students that they will continue working through Holly's problem in the next lesson and that they should be thinking about what kind of quality of work they are presently turning in in their own classes. In the next class, tell them to be prepared to give some examples of what prevents them from turning in quality work.

MEET HOLLY HOOCARES

Problem

This is Holly Hoocares. See if you can figure out her problem at school.

> It was supposed to be done in pencil?
> Well, all I had was a pen.
> And you say we were supposed to <u>add</u> these numbers instead of subtract? Well, I didn't bother to look at that + sign all over the paper.
> Now you're telling me I skipped 3 rows ???
> But look - I did the whole page in just 5 minutes. I did it FAST! And <u>I did most of it!</u>

> Yeah..... most of it wrong !!

Behavior (B)

What behavior is a problem for Holly?

Consequences ←(B)→

What are some consequences of this behavior?

Choices ⊕

What other behavior choices does Holly have?

HOLLY'S GOAL

Goal

Here are some ideas for goals for Holly. Look them over carefully and choose the one you think might help Holly start to be a better student. Why did you pick that goal?

☐   **Goal A:**   I will turn in all my assignments without ANY mistakes for the rest of my life!

☐   **Goal B:**   I will turn in all my math assignments in ink.

☐   **Goal C:**   I will pick *one* class to start with and improve my work in that class by working carefully.

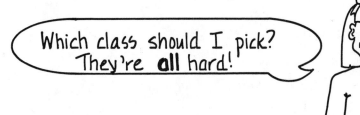

☐   **Goal D:**   I will get an "A+" in English class.

HOLLY'S PLAN

Plan

    Here are Holly's ideas for being a better math student. Which ideas do you think would be helpful for Holly?

Plan A

I will make sure I understand the directions before starting.

Reducing fractions? Sounds like a new diet. I'd better ask about this.

Plan B

I will follow the directions while doing the work.

At the end of each row, I'll stop and review the directions.

Plan C

I will have my sister, Perfect Patty, do my math homework.

Don't make your 7's look like 2's. Work carefully Sis!

Plan D

I will do the problems in order so I don't skip any.

If I come to a hard one, I'll circle it and come back to it later.

Plan E

I will work as quickly as possible.

I'll be done before my brain stops working!

Plan F

I will check over the work when I am finished.

Time to check over the circled problems.

CAREFUL WORK MEANS BETTER GRADES

Keeping Track

What are the things Holly needs to know or do to carry out her plan? Put an X in front of each item below:

_____ a. She needs to understand how to do the assignment.

_____ b. She needs to understand the directions.

_____ c. She needs to have a pen.

_____ d. She needs to follow the directions through the assignment.

_____ e. She needs to stop and get a drink of water after every three problems.

_____ f. She needs to start at the beginning of the assignment and work to the end.

_____ g. She needs to do her math in study hall.

_____ h. She needs to have her sister do the hard problems.

_____ i. She needs to skip the hard problems and come back to them at the end.

_____ j. She needs to remember to check over her work at the end.

Reward

Holly knows she will have to try hard to use her plan and work carefully. To help herself work hard, she is going to reward herself when she reaches her goal. Here are some things Holly could use to reward herself:

buying makeup.....

buying makeup....

buying more makeup.

When I reach my goal, I will reward myself by _____.

Summary

Holly has a problem with _____.

She has set a goal of getting an average score of _____% on her daily math assignments for _____ week(s).

Her plan is to _____ the directions, _____ the directions, and _____ her work at the end.

HOLLY'S QUESTION CARD AND
DAILY GRADE CARD

Question Card

BEFORE:	DURING:	AFTER:
Do I understand the directions?	Am I following the directions?	Did I check over my work for mistakes?

Daily Grade Card

DAY/DATE	MATH GRADE
Monday	_____
Tuesday	_____
Wednesday	_____
Thursday	_____
Friday	_____
Weekly average: _____ %	

Holly's math grades before using her plan:

Week 1		*Week 2*	
Monday	70%	Monday	53%
Tuesday	63%	Tuesday	86%
Wednesday	91%	Wednesday	77%
Thursday	82%	Thursday	42%
Friday	77%	Friday	80%
Weekly average: _____%		Weekly average _____%	

Lesson 30   HOLLY'S GOAL AND PLAN

Overview

This lesson gives the student an opportunity to examine possible goals and plans for Holly. While some of the goals and plans may contain some workable ideas, the best goal and plan is one that is practical and within reach for someone like Holly, who has never been a careful student. Students should realize that no one can change overnight, but that taking positive steps toward becoming a better student is as important as the final product. It takes time!

Lesson Objectives

- Students will choose an appropriate goal from several possible goals and explain why that goal is most appropriate for the given situation.
- Students will identify appropriate ideas that can be formulated into a plan and explain why the ideas are most appropriate for the given situation.

Teacher Preparation

Copies of Worksheets 29-2 and 29-3 should already be included in the students' packet of materials.

Lesson Plan

1. Review material covered in the previous lesson by asking students to summarize Holly's problem behavior, consequences, and choices. Ask students to state what they concluded would be a better choice of behaviors for Holly (to do quality work in school).

2. Ask students to locate the packet (Worksheets 29-1 through 29-5) from the previous day and to locate Worksheet 29-2, "Holly's Goal."

3. Direct students' attention to the comments at the top. Explain that they will be considering several goals for Holly and will choose the one that they think is the most appropriate. Discuss the following questions:

   Goal A
   a. What problem do you see with this goal? (everyone makes mistakes)
   b. Do you think this goal is unrealistic? Why? (yes, there are some subjects that are difficult for some people)
   c. How do you feel about this goal? (answers will vary)

Goal B

a. Will doing her work in ink make Holly a better student? (no, probably has nothing to do with it)

b. What problems do you see with this goal? (math shouldn't be done in ink)

c. How do you feel about this goal? (answers will vary)

Goal C

a. Why would picking only one class help Holly? (so she doesn't get overwhelmed and frustrated by trying to improve everything at once)

b. Should Holly pick an easy class or a difficult class? (probably a difficult class so she could see more improvement; if the techniques work with a difficult class, they will probably also work with an easier class)

c. How do you feel about this goal? (answers will vary)

Goal D

a. Is getting an "A+" a good thing to strive for? (yes, but is it realistic?)

b. How do you think Holly will feel if she doesn't even come close to getting an "A"? (discouraged)

c. How do you feel about this goal? (answers will vary)

Conclude that Goal C is probably the most reasonable goal for Holly because it is not overwhelming (only one class will be considered), she mentions "improving" (that does not necessarily mean getting an "A+"), and she sees that there is a connection between working carefully and being a better student.

4. Direct students' attention to the plans on Worksheet 29-3. Call on volunteers to read the comments at the top and the six plans that are highlighted on the worksheet. Make sure students understand that more than one idea can be combined into a plan. Also make sure that students take note of the fact that Holly will be working on improving her *math* assignments. Discussion questions are

Plan A

a. How could this idea help Holly? (she would understand what to do before she wastes time and effort doing something wrong)

b. What do you think of this plan for Holly? (helpful)

Plan B

a. How would this idea help Holly? (if she keeps on following the directions, her work will be correct)

b. What do you think of this idea? (helpful)

Plan C

a. Will this idea help Holly get better grades? (might)

b. How would this idea hurt Holly? (she might get caught, she wouldn't learn anything)

c. What do you think of this idea? (not good)

Plan D

a. How could this idea help Holly? (she wouldn't spend time puzzling over something she doesn't know how to do)

b. How could this idea hurt Holly? (she might forget to come back to the circled problems)

c. What do you think of this idea? (helpful)

Plan E

a. Do you think working quickly would help Holly's math? (it probably wouldn't; speed would probably result in more mistakes)

b. What happens sometimes when you work too quickly? (overlook details, make mistakes)

c. What do you think of this idea? (not good)

Plan F

a. What does "checking work over" mean? (might mean redoing a few problems, scanning for circled or omitted problems, or making sure the paper looks neat)

b. What if Holly is not careful about checking over her work carefully? (she'll overlook the obvious mistakes)

c. What do you think of this idea? (good)

5. REVIEW: (a) Ask students to summarize Holly's goal. Ask why it is acceptable to start with only one class rather than trying to improve in all classes at the same time. (b) Ask students to summarize the four ideas that would help make a good plan for Holly to follow (A, B, D, F). (c) Ask students to offer suggestions of their own for proofreading their assignments—if they have found it to be worth the extra time it takes, and what specific techniques they may have used. (d) Tell students to file this packet in their folders.

6. ASSIGNMENT: Inform students that on the next day, they will work on keeping track of Holly's math assignments. For their assignment, they should decide on exactly what kind of grades they think Holly should be getting to be an "improved" student. Assume that Holly is a "C" student now. How much improvement do they think is reasonable for Holly to expect in math by using her plan?

Lesson 31 USING A QUESTION CARD AND DAILY GRADE CARD

Overview

In this lesson, students will be presented with specific aids for carrying out Holly's plan. In particular, they will be exposed to a question card that Holly uses before, during, and after working on her math assignment. The card has three questions that Holly asks herself to cue herself to stay on task throughout the assignment. The other aid is a Daily Grade Card, which is simply a chart for Holly to put the daily assignment scores on with a space to tally the average weekly score at the bottom. Students will consider an appropriate reward for Holly and summarize the plan.

Lesson Objectives

- Students will identify necessary subtasks for carrying out a specified plan for changing behavior.
- Students will identify an appropriate reward for reaching a goal.
- Students will state the purpose of a Question Card and Daily Grade Card and demonstrate the intended use of each.

Teacher Preparation

Copies of Worksheets 29-4 and 29-5 should already be included in the packet of materials previously distributed to students.

Lesson Plan

1. Review material previously discussed by asking students the following questions:

    What is Holly's basic problem? (failing to turn in quality work)

    What is Holly's goal? (to improve her math grades)

    What is Holly's plan? (to more carefully follow directions and to proofread her work)

2. Inform students that now they will refine the goal and plan to be more specific. As mentioned in the previous lesson's assignment, students will be asked their opinion about how much improvement they think Holly

could be capable of in her math class. After considering students' opinions, direct students to the conclusion that if Holly was getting "C's" without doing her work carefully, perhaps she should try for a "B" average. That would not demand a radical improvement to achieve success, but it would certainly indicate that her plan was working. Specify an 80% average for one week.

3. Ask students to locate the packet of Worksheets 29-1 through 29-5 from their folders and turn to Worksheet 29-4, "Careful Work Means Better Grades."

4. Ask students if they think there is a connection between careful work and better grades. Try to lead students to the conclusion that some basic ability has to be involved for good grades, but that effort and giving a little extra time and consideration to being careful can prevent needless mistakes and therefore improve grades.

5. Ask a student volunteer to read the "Keeping Track" section of the worksheet. Give students a few minutes to complete the checklist and discuss the items. Answers are

    Holly will need to know or do *a, b, d, f* (probably), *i* (probably), and *j*. Discuss the benefits of including the items.

6. Direct students' attention to the "Reward" section of the worksheet. Students will probably suggest some type of makeup as a reward for Holly.

7. Direct students' attention to the "Summary" section and allow them a few minutes to complete the sentences. Answers are

    Holly has a problem with (doing quality/careful work).

    She has set a goal of getting an average score of (80%) on her daily math assignments for one (week).

    Her plan is to (understand) the directions, (follow) the directions, and (proofread/check) her work at the end.

8. Direct students' attention to Worksheet 29-5, "Holly's Question Card and Daily Grade Card." Inform students that Holly is going to use these two cards to assist her in following her plan.

9. Discuss the questions on the Question Card. Ask for student volunteers to read the before/during/after questions and comment on why each question would be helpful to Holly.

10. Discuss the Daily Grade Card. Be sure that students understand where each math score will go (on the line opposite the day of the assignment) and that the number should be expressed as a percentage. Make sure students understand how to calculate the weekly average at the bottom of the card.

11. Allow students time to work the two problems at the bottom of the worksheet if you feel that some practice in averaging math scores would be beneficial. Answers are

    Week 1: 76%
    Week 2: 67%

12. REVIEW: (a) Ask students to summarize Holly's method of keeping track of her behavior. (b) Ask students to summarize Holly's plan (using a Question Card and a Daily Grade Card) and goal (averaging 80% on daily math assignments for one week). (c) Tell students to file this packet in their folders.

13. ASSIGNMENT: Inform students they will be working with Holly's question card tomorrow and that as they have opportunity throughout the day, they should give them a try to see if they are helpful.

Lesson 32 PRACTICING HOLLY'S PLAN

Overview

Students will "observe" Holly as she works through her math assignment using her question card. Students are to decide whether or not Holly is using the questions correctly to complete the task. On the first day, Monday, Holly uses the card and questions accurately. Students are exposed to Holly "talking to herself" or talking through the problems. Self-questioning can be very effective when students feel free to answer themselves, especially proceeding step by step through the procedure. On the second day, Tuesday, Holly hurries through her math and makes some mistakes. This example shows how Holly catches herself and realizes the need to rely on the question card.

Lesson Objective

- Students will view examples of a student-model using a questioning technique to complete an assignment and decide whether or not the model was following the plan accurately.

Teacher Preparation

Make enough copies of Worksheet 32-1, "Monday's Math Assignment," and Worksheet 32-2, "Tuesday's Math Assignment," for your students.

Lesson Plan

1. Review previous material by asking students what Holly's two aids are for her plan. Ask students for their experiences in using the questioning technique on their assignments.

2. Distribute Worksheet 32-1 to students. Ask for a student volunteer to read the comments at the top. Make sure that students are familiar with the abbreviated version of the Question Card and can state the entire question for each of the three parts.

3. Ask for a student volunteer to read Box 1 and decide whether or not Holly was using her plan. (Yes, it is the "before" stage, and she consulted her card to make sure that she understood the directions.)

4. Continue the procedure with the remaining boxes. The answers are

> Box 2—Yes, Holly is in the "during" stage, and at the end of the first row she stopped to ask herself if she was still following the directions.

> Box 3—Yes, she decided to circle one that she wasn't sure of and remembered to check to see if she was still following the directions at the end of the row.

> Box 4—Yes, Holly is in the "after" stage of the assignment and remembered to catch herself and ask herself the final question. She then rechecked several problems and made sure she worked the circled problems again.

5. Distribute Worksheet 32-2 to students. Call students' attention to the question card at the top and ask for student volunteers to read the comments in each of the boxes and decide whether or not Holly is using her plan. The answers are

> Box 1—No, Holly isn't sure what the ( ) are for, but she doesn't take the time to ask; she goes ahead and begins the assignment.

> Box 2—Yes, now Holly understands the procedure and continues.

> Box 3—No, Holly didn't complete the entire assignment; she did not follow the entire directions.

> Box 4—Yes, she remembered to check over her work before handing it in.

6. Ask students to discuss any questions or comments about Holly's use of the question card and technique.

7. REVIEW: (a) Ask students to summarize this lesson's activities, specifically stating the questions for each stage of the assignment and how Holly handled her assignments on the two days. (b) Tell students to file the worksheets in their folders. (c) Inform students that they will have information to help them complete the rest of Holly's daily grade card tomorrow.

8. ASSIGNMENT: You may want to have students begin keeping a record of their current daily grades in a specific subject. This information can be used later to establish a baseline for students so that they can decide how much improvement in that subject they would like to achieve.

MONDAY'S MATH ASSIGNMENT

Watch as Holly works on her math assignment and decide if she is using her plan.

BEFORE—DURING—AFTER
Understand? Follow? Check Over?

1. Is Holly using her plan? _____

2. Is Holly using her plan? _____

3. Is Holly using her plan? _____

4. Is Holly using her plan? _____

TUESDAY'S MATH ASSIGNMENT

Today, Holly has a math assignment with two-step problems. Watch as Holly works on her math today and decide if she is using her plan.

> BEFORE—DURING—AFTER
> Understand? Follow? Check Over?

1. Is Holly using her plan? _____

2. Is Holly using her plan? _____

3. Is Holly using her plan? _____

4. Is Holly using her plan? _____

Lesson 33   HOW DID HOLLY DO?

Overview

Students are given information about Holly's math scores on her daily assignments so that they can complete the Daily Grade Card for one week and calculate Holly's average. Evaluation questions are provided for students to consider based on Holly's experiences with the plan and her math assignments. Finally, additional assignments for other subjects are provided so that students can begin thinking about how they could adapt the questioning technique to fit other types of subjects.

Lesson Objectives

- Students will accurately complete a Daily Grade Card and calculate the weekly average score.
- Students will evaluate this plan for Holly by determining whether or not it worked for Holly.
- Students will write or state appropriate questions that could be used to do more careful work on other types of subjects.

Teacher Preparation

1. Make enough copies of Worksheet 33-1, "More Math," Worksheet 33-2, "Evaluation Form—How Did Holly Do?," and Worksheet 33-3, "Doing Quality Work on All Assignments," for your students.
2. If you think your students may have difficulty filling in the columns of the Daily Grade Card or calculating the average score for the week, you might want to copy the Daily Grade Card form on the chalkboard and complete it as your students complete theirs on the worksheet.
3. Worksheet 33-4, "Sample Daily Grade Card and Question Card," is available if you want your students to use it for the related assignments project.

Lesson Plan

1. Ask for student comments about their experiences using the questioning technique with their classes.
2. If assigned, ask students how their record keeping of grades in a designated class is coming along.

3. Explain that in today's lesson, they will see how Holly did with her plan and math assignments for the rest of the week, evaluate how the plan worked for her, and think about how they could use this plan with other subjects.

4. Distribute Worksheet 33-1 to students. Ask for student volunteers to read the information and allow students time to complete the Daily Grade Card. You may want to complete this form on the board while students follow along step by step. Answers are

Monday	89%
Tuesday	95%
Wednesday	79%
Thursday	82%
Friday	91%
Average Score:	87%
1. 87%	
2. Yes	
3. Yes	

5. Ask students for their conclusions about Holly's plan and her improved grades.

6. Distribute Worksheet 33-2 to students. Ask for student volunteers to read the comments at the top and allow time for students to calculate Holly's scores for week 2. (83%; yes, she made it)

7. Call on student volunteers to read and answer the evaluation questions on the remainder of the worksheet. Suggested answers include

1. Yes, she had trouble remembering to use the technique.

2. Yes, once she got used to using them, they helped her stay on task.

3. If you don't understand the directions, you may do the entire assignment wrong.

4. Yes, after she asked, she did the problems correctly.

5. If you stop following the directions, you will do it incorrectly.

6. She stopped at the end of each row of problems.

7. She circled them so she wouldn't spend time puzzling over them, but wouldn't forget to come back to them at the end.

8. Opinion (some students may feel that erasing the circle makes the paper messy).

9. Holly asked herself if she remembered to check her work over.

10. She redid several problems and checked for any circled problems.

11–13. Opinions.

8. Distribute Worksheet 33-3. You may want to assign this to small groups or as a homework assignment. Students are given situations in classes other than math to develop a question card appropriate for the situation presented. Worksheet 33-4 is available to use on this assignment or for the next lesson in which students will actually record their grades for a class. Suggested questions for the assignments are

English

a. Do I understand the assignment?
   Do I have 25 sentences?
   Did I circle the subject for each sentence?
   Did I underline the predicate for each sentence?
   Did I check over my work before handing it in?

b. Did I write three paragraphs?
   Did I use capital letters correctly?
   Did I use punctuation correctly?
   Are all my sentences complete?
   Is the assignment in ink?
   Does the paper look neat?

c. Did I list two or three reasons in this note?
Did I use cursive writing?

Social Studies

a. Do I have the correct page located in my book?
Do I understand the directions for doing this page?
Did I write the word correctly?
Did I underline each word?
Did I use each word in a sentence?
Did I write the definition for each word?

b. Do I have the correct page located in my book?
Did I answer all five questions?
Did I answer using complete sentences?

Science

a. Do I have ten insects in mind to study?
Does my assignment look like a chart?
Did the chart indicate what part of the country each insect is found in?
Did the chart indicate the lifespan of each insect?
Did the chart indicate reasons why each insect is harmful/helpful to people?

b. Do I have eight different kinds of seeds?
Did I follow the directions about displaying the seeds?
Does the chart describe where I found the seeds?
Does the chart tell how the seed got to each place?
Does the chart tell what kind of seed it is?

9. REVIEW: (a) Have students offer their opinions as to Holly's plan, goal, and behavior change. Ask what problems they saw that might affect them if they were to use the plan. (b) Explain to students that they will begin working on doing quality work in one class in particular and that they will do some record keeping like Holly did. (c) Tell students to file their worksheets in their folders.

10. ASSIGNMENTS: (a) If you have not already done so, have students come prepared with one class in mind for which they will do better work. (b) If students are already recording daily grades for a class, remind them to continue to do so. (You may want to take a look at their charts to make sure they are keeping up and filling them out accurately.)

MORE MATH

Holly used her plan on her math assignments for the rest of the week. Use the information below to fill out Holly's Daily Grade Card and see if she reached her goal.

Day/Date	Math Grade
Monday	_____
Tuesday	_____
Wednesday	_____
Thursday	_____
Friday	_____
Weekly average:	_____ %

On Monday, Holly worked on addition problems. She used her plan very carefully and got a score of 89%.

Tuesday, she had some trouble figuring out what to do with ( ) problems, but after she understood the directions and checked over her work, she got a 95% on that paper.

Wednesday was a hard day. Holly worked on fractions. She understood what to do, but didn't always remember to go back and work the ones that she circled. Her score was 79%.

On Thursday, the class worked on story problems. At the end of each problem, Holly checked to make sure she had followed the directions. Her score was 82% on that paper.

Friday was a multiplication speed drill. She understood what to do, followed the directions, and got a 91% on the assignment.

1. What was Holly's average score for this week? _____ %

2. Did she average 80% or better? _____

3. Did she reach her goal for this week? _____

EVALUATION FORM—HOW DID HOLLY DO?

These are Holly's math assignment scores for Week 2. If she wanted to have at least an 80% average for the week for her goal, did she make it?

Day/Date	Math Grade
Monday	72%
Tuesday	69%
Wednesday	100%
Thursday	88%
Friday	87%
Weekly average	_____%

Evaluation Questions

1. Did Holly have any trouble using her plan at first?

2. Do you think the questions helped Holly remember what to do?

3. Why is it important to understand the directions before starting the assignment?

4. Did understanding the directions make a difference on Holly's assignments?

5. Why is it important to keep following the directions?

6. When did Holly stop to ask herself if she was still following the directions?

7. Why did Holly circle the problems she was having trouble with?

8. Do you think that is a good idea or do you have another idea?

9. What did Holly ask herself at the end of the assignment?

10. How did Holly check over her work?

11. Do you have other ideas for checking over your work?

12. Do you think this is a good plan to use to be a better student?

13. What are other ways that you can help yourself be a better student by doing careful work?

Name _____ Date _____

DOING QUALITY WORK ON ALL ASSIGNMENTS

How could Holly use her Question Card to help her do quality work on assignments for other classes? What questions would be helpful *before, during,* and *after* the assignment?

English Assignments

1. Write 25 sentences. Circle the subject and underline the predicate in each sentence.

2. Write three paragraphs about something you like to do. Make sure you use correct capital letters, punctuation, and have complete sentences. Use ink and erase mistakes carefully.

3. Write a thank-you note for something you received for your birthday. Make sure you use cursive writing. Give at least two reasons why you liked the gift.

Social Studies Assignments

1. Look up the ten vocabulary words at the end of Chapter 1. Write the word, underline it, use it in a sentence, and copy the definition.

2. Answer the five questions at the end of Chapter 3 about the Civil War. Use a complete sentence to answer each question. All the answers you need are in the chapter.

Science Assignments

1. Use your science book to look up the habits of ten insects. Make a chart to tell what part of the country each insect could be found in, how long each insect usually lives, and how it is helpful or harmful to man.

2. Collect at least eight different kinds of seeds. Display them on a posterboard chart and describe where you found them, how you think it might have gotten there, and what kind of seed it is.

SAMPLE DAILY GRADE CARD
AND QUESTION CARD

Daily Grade Card

Day/Date	Math Grade
Monday	_____
Tuesday	_____
Wednesday	_____
Thursday	_____
Friday	_____
Weekly average:	_____ %

BEFORE	DURING	AFTER

Lesson 34 APPLICATION—CARE ABOUT QUALITY

Overview

Now that students have had practice with the techniques that Holly Hoocares used to improve her math assignments, they should be ready to apply this knowledge to improving their own schoolwork. Your considerations for this project should include

1. Do you want all students to monitor their assignments for the same subject? In some cases, daily assignments are not given. For the purpose of practice, it may be helpful to target a class for which assignments are given frequently.

2. Do you want all students to use the same questions? Some students may be able to proofread their work more adeptly than others, while slower or more careless students may need more questions and more stopping points to check over their work and monitor themselves *while* working, not merely at the end.

3. Do you want students to show the same level of improvement for their goals? Since students will not all be at the same starting point (percentagewise), you need to decide what would be an appropriate level of improvement for each student to attain (for example, one letter grade or five percentage points).

Students should be encouraged to bring in assignments from any classes on which they have gotten a good grade or good comments. Keep in mind that for some students, a "D" is a good grade! It is important to encourage students to accept small successes as steps in the right direction and that steadily improving in this area is just as valuable as experiencing overnight success. Students should be encouraged to share their observations about each other's assignments and suggestions for improving the appearance of work turned in. Often the constructive criticism of a peer is more meaningful and better taken than are comments from the teacher. Examples of actual assignments (with names removed) can be examined and evaluated as a class to determine what is looked for on a paper and what is important. Simply getting the right answer is not the entire job!

Students should carry out their individual projects for at least two weeks. At the end of the first week, you may want to ask for volunteers to share their specific successes and problems with their projects. If students are not improving on their assignments, the problem needs to be located and addressed.

Students will also need to practice the self-questioning technique. It is important that the right questions are asked of the assignment and that honest answers are given. It may be helpful to have students role-play situations in which they use self-questioning to move themselves methodically through an assignment.

Lesson Objectives

- Students will devise a plan for improving their quality of assignments in a specific subject.
- Students will set and reach a realistic goal for their project of turning in quality work.
- Students will accurately record their scores from daily assignments on a Daily Grade Card.
- Students will demonstrate familiarity with the use of self-question techniques by appropriately asking and responding to questions about their assignment and quality of work on that assignment.

Teacher Preparation

1. Make enough copies of Worksheet 34-1, "Student Worksheet," for your students.
2. You may want to run off additional copies of Worksheet 33-4, "Sample Daily Grade Card and Question Card," for students to familiarize themselves with as they complete the worksheet.
3. You may also want to copy the following symbols on the chalkboard to refer to as the different sections on the worksheet are discussed.

Lesson Plan

1. Inform students that since Holly Hoocares successfully is on her way to becoming a better student, their attention can now be directed toward their own assignments. Explain that they will be formulating their own plan and goal in today's lesson and will soon begin carrying out a plan similar to Holly's.
2. Distribute Worksheet 34-1 (two pages) to students.
3. Discuss the questions on the worksheet and allow students time to record their opinions and/or commitments to making a suitable plan and goal.

a. Question 3: If you have asked students to begin recording their scores in a particular class, you would probably want them to continue working toward improvement in that class.

b. Question 4: Again, if students have recorded their scores, they should have some idea as to their objective performance in terms of a number or grade. If not, you may want to assign the additional task to students of talking to the teacher of whatever class is targeted and finding out what the past week's average score has been.

c. Question 6: Answers may vary, depending on the consequences that individual teachers place on careless work. You may want to list the various responses that are given.

d. Question 7: Have students affirm that it is *their* responsibility to turn in careful work.

e. Question 9: Direct students to setting a goal that includes a numerical value, for example, a percentage of correct answers, or 85% of assignments that are passing, and so on.

f. Question 10: Have students stay within a two-week time frame for reaching their goal. If their plan doesn't begin to show results in one week, an additional week probably won't benefit them, and they should reevaluate the plan.

g. Question 11: Students should simply state that they are going to change their behavior by turning in quality assignments.

h. Question 12: Students should specify what specifically they will do differently to change their behavior; for example, use a question card on the assignment, ask for help when stuck rather than just sit there, work more slowly, work faster, and so on.

i. Question 14: Students note what items or forms they will need to prepare.

j. Question 15: Students may want to refer to Worksheet 33-4 to devise their own forms or to use with or without modifications.

k. Question 16: This is a summary statement to help students keep their goal in mind. An example might read: "At the end of *two weeks*, I will look at my *Daily Grade Card* and see whether or not I have *gotten better grades on my assignments*. If my percentage is *90%* or higher, I have reached my goal."

l. Question 17: For additional incentive, you may want to offer a class reward for students who have reached their goal.

4. Allow time for any specific questions, comments, or problems with the worksheet and development of their plans and goals.

5. Tell students to file their worksheets in their folders, except for the form(s) they will be using to record their assignment scores and/or use for questioning themselves about their assignments.

6. Decide when your class will actually begin carrying out their projects. You may want to allow a day or two for all students to make and/or assemble needed materials.

7. Class time should be set aside daily to address questions or comments that arise relative to doing more careful work. Remind students that they will share their findings with the class when all students have participated in the project for one or two weeks. Keep the following points in mind:

   a. Students may expect to see overnight success. Remind them that *effort* is required to see changes and that as long as they keep working on establishing careful work habits and proofreading skills, they will improve.

   b. Use the success of other students' work as models for the others. A student may not be particularly impressed with Patty Perfect's scores going from "A−" to "A+", but seeing Amy Average's scores go from a "D+" to a "C−" might make an impression that can be identified with.

   c. Show students lots of examples of careful and careless work and have them specify what criteria might be used to evaluate that assignment. In math, for example, a careful paper might involve neatly written numbers, circled answers, few erasures, and so on. In English, however, a grader may look for cursive handwriting, neat letters, use of a pen rather than pencil, complete sentences, and so on. Often students are more severe critics of what constitutes a "good" paper than are teachers!

STUDENT WORKSHEET

1. *Behavior:* Is this behavior, doing quality work, something that would help make you a better student?

   (B) _____

2. Do you work carefully in all your classes? _____

3. Is there a particular class that you have more difficulty with than other classes? _____

   What? _____

4. What kind of grades do you get on assignments in your most difficult class? _____

5. If you did more careful work, do you think you could get better grades? _____

6. *Consequences:* What are the consequences when you turn in assignments that you didn't work

   on carefully? _____

   _____

7. *Choices:* Do you *have* to turn in careless assignments? _____

8. What is another choice that you have? _____

9. *Goal:* What goal will you set for yourself?

   My goal is to: _____

10. How long do you think it will take you to reach your goal?

    _____

11. How are you going to change your behavior to reach your goal?

    _____

12. *Plan:* What are some ideas for your plan to reach your goal?

    I could _____

    I could _____

    I could _____

13. Choose a plan. I pick _____

14. What do you need to do or get to carry out the plan? _____

_____

_____

_____

15. How will you *keep track* of your behavior and plan? (You can use a Question Card and Daily

    Grade Card like Holly's or make your own.) _____

     _____

    _____

    _____

16. How will you know when you have reached your goal?

    At the end of _____, I will look at my _____

    　　　　　　　　(how long?)　　　　　　　　　　　　　(cards, chart)

    and see whether or not I have _____.

    　　　　　　　　　　　　　　　(what behavior are you changing?)

    If my percentage is _____ or higher, I have reached my goal.

    　　　　　　　　(what %)

17. *Reward:* How will you reward yourself? _____

    ✳　　When will you reward yourself? _____

    This plan and goal will be evaluated on _____.

    　　　　　　　　　　　　　　　　　　　　　(date)

Lesson 35   EVALUATION OF YOUR PROJECT

Overview

After students have participated in their project for one or two weeks, they should share their experiences and conclusions with the class. This may be done on a volunteer basis if desired, since some students may be hesitant to share their grades with the class. While not all students will have made glowing improvements in scores, each student will have had some experience with the relationship between directed effort on an assignment and the corresponding grade. Keep in mind that this is still a learning experience for students and that, even though they have a long way to go, they have made strides in terms of improving skills and/or increasing their awareness of what is involved in doing quality work on assignments.

Lesson Objectives

- Students will determine whether or not they have reached their goal.
- Students will specify modifications for their plan to improve it if it were to be continued.

Teacher Preparation

The evaluation form for this lesson is the same as Worksheet 28-1, "Evaluation Questions." Make enough copies of this worksheet for your students.

Lesson Plan

1. Have students assemble all paperwork that was used in carrying out their project (for example, assignments, Daily Grade Card, Question Card, etc.).
2. Distribute Worksheet 28-1 to students.
3. Inform students that now that they have worked on their plans for awhile, they will evaluate them to see if they are working or not and how well they are working. Remind students that even if they feel as if their plan didn't work at all, they still learned something from it and that sharing that information with others can help other students to avoid the same mistakes.
4. Discuss questions on the worksheet. If some students do not want to share specific information with the class, you may have them respond to more general questions about the plans of other students. All students should complete the evaluation form according to their own projects.

5. Conclude the discussion by asking for student comments about the value of the project for them.

6. Tell students to file their worksheets and other paperwork in their folders.

7. You may want to grade the projects of the students based on their adherence to the plan, achievement of the goal, effort, and actual behavior change.

Lesson 36 DUDLEY DREAMALOT'S PROBLEM

Overview

Dudley Dreamalot is a boy who attends class in body, but whose mind is miles away. He would rather daydream about what he'd like to be doing in his free time than pay attention to what's going on in class. He's the kind of student who may not be actively disruptive, but he doesn't contribute anything to the class because he's not participating. If anything, he slows the pace of the class because he doesn't know what page the class is on, what the directions were, or what went on during class.

Students should again be given a five-page packet containing the outline of Dudley's behavior, consequences, choices, goal, plan, recordkeeping technique, reward, and summary paragraph.

The information should be reviewed daily and applications made to the students' own classes as much as possible. The eventual outcome is for students to apply Dudley's techniques for improving his participation in class to their own situations.

Lesson Objectives

- Students will identify a hypothetical student's behavior problem.
- Students will identify at least two consequences of that behavior.
- Students will identify at least two behavioral choices that could be selected instead of the problem behavior.

Teacher Preparation

1. Make enough copies of Worksheets 36-1 through 36-5 for your students. These worksheets can be collated and stapled to present to students as an entire packet.
2. Copy the following on the chalkboard:

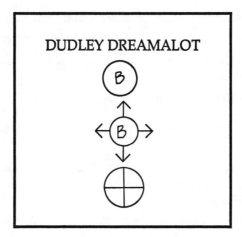

Lesson Plan

1. Introduce the lesson by stating the class is now going to consider the problem of Dudley Dreamalot and ask for any guesses as to what his problem might be.

2. Distribute the packet of worksheets to students.

3. Instruct the students to look at the first page of the packet, Worksheet 36-1, "Meet Dudley Dreamalot." Call on a volunteer to read Dudley's comments.

4. Direct students' attention to the board. As you discuss the questions on the worksheet, refer to the symbols.

5. Direct students' attention to the "Behavior" section of the worksheet. Ask students to identify what behavior is preventing Dudley from being a better student. Ideas may include not listening to the teacher, thinking about playing softball, or daydreaming.

6. Summarize students' responses by selecting "not participating in class" as Dudley's problem. If students are confused by this, explain that even though Dudley was sitting at a desk in the class, he was not receiving any information from the teacher (because of his daydreaming) and not giving out any information (not answering a question). Explain that even if a student sits and listens to what's going on in class, if that student doesn't give back any information to let the teacher know he or she understands what's going on and is keeping up with the class, that student is not an active, participating member of the class. You may want to write this on the board next to ⒷⒷ.

7. Direct students' attention to the "Consequences" section of the worksheet. Ask students to identify some possible consequences that may happen because Dudley doesn't participate in class. Ideas may include

Dudley will not understand how to do the homework for that class.

Dudley will not be listening when something interesting is discussed.

Dudley will be embarrassed by not knowing the answer to an easy question.

Dudley will not do well on the test.

Ask students to consider whether any of the consequences are good ones for Dudley.

8. Direct students' attention to the "Choices" section of their worksheet. Explain that Dudley does not have to daydream during his classes; he chooses to. Even though Dudley may not particularly be interested in a certain class, he has an obligation as a student to try to master the material. Ask students to give some ideas for other choices that Dudley has for participating in class. Ideas may include

Dudley could choose to think about the class instead of softball.

Dudley could take notes on what the teacher is saying.

Dudley could look at the teacher during class and have his book open to the correct page all the time.

9. Ask students to list at least two choices that Dudley has and write them on their worksheet. Tell them to put a star by the one they think is the best choice for Dudley. (*Idea:* Pick one that mentions Dudley's responsibility for paying attention in class.)

10. REVIEW: (a) Ask students to summarize Dudley's problem behavior, some consequences of that behavior, and a good alternative choice of behaviors. (b) Tell students to file this packet in their folders.

11. ASSIGNMENT: Inform students that they will be considering how to help Dudley participate in his classes. As they go through their various classes, ask students to think about which classes are hard to pay attention in, why, and what they think might make it easier to participate in that class.

MEET DUDLEY DREAMALOT

Problem ?

Here is Dudley Dreamalot in his science class. What do you think his problem is?

Behavior (B)

What behavior is keeping Dudley from being a better student?

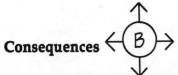

Consequences

What are some consequences of this behavior?

Choices ⊕

What other behavior choices does Dudley have?

DUDLEY'S GOAL

Goal

Here are some ideas for goals to help Dudley participate in school. Which one do you think is the best for Dudley? Why?

_____

☐ Goal A: I will pay attention to everything that my teachers say in every class all day long, every day.

I'm not going to miss a thing!

_____

☐ Goal B: I will raise my hand once each day to answer a question in one class.

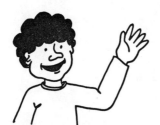

The answer is 20! Now I can go back to sleep!

_____

☐ Goal C: I will go to every class every day.

I'm here. What a thrill.

_____

☐ Goal D: I will do at least four things every day in one class to show that I am participating.

I can raise my hand— but what else?

_____

DUDLEY'S PLAN

Plan

Here are some ideas for making a plan for Dudley to participate in his classes. Which ideas do you think would help him the most?

PARTICIPATING IN CLASS

Keeping Track

What are the things Dudley needs to know or do to carry out his plan? Put an X in front of each item.

____ a. He needs to be ready to participate in class by having his materials.

____ b. He needs to go to school even on days when he is sick.

____ c. He needs to raise his hand to ask and answer questions.

____ d. He needs to watch the clock.

____ e. He needs to watch the teacher.

____ f. He needs to type his notes every night at home.

____ h. He needs to write down important things about the class.

____ i. He needs to get an "A" on every assignment so that his teacher will like him.

Reward ✳

Dudley often finds that he is late to softball practice because he is doing the work that he could have done at school but he chose to daydream instead. Knowing that Dudley likes softball a lot, what might be an appropriate reward for Dudley to work for?

_____

Summary

Dudley has a problem with _____.

He has set a goal of giving himself _____ during class to show that
    he is actively participating in the class.

He will work on this goal for _____ week(s).

To reach his goal, he wants to have _____ in his _____ class each day.

His plan is to use a _____ to make sure he is participating in the

    class _____, _____, and _____ the class.

USING A CHECKLIST

Class _____ Week of _____

BEFORE CLASS	Mon.	Tues.	Wed.	Thurs.	Fri.
1. Materials?	____	____	____	____	____
2. Ready?	____	____	____	____	____
DURING CLASS					
3. Raise hand?	____	____	____	____	____
4. Look at teacher?	____	____	____	____	____
AFTER CLASS					
5. Notes?	____	____	____	____	____
6. Summary?	____	____	____	____	____
Total (out of 6)	____	____	____	____	____

Try This:

1. On Monday, Dudley forgot to bring a pencil: Should he give himself a ✓ for #1? _____

2. On Tuesday, Dudley raised his hand—not once, not twice, but three times! Should he give

   himself three ✓s? _____

3. On Wednesday, Dudley was late to class, forgot his books, and did not take any notes. What

   would his score be on that day? _____

4. On Thursday, Dudley took a lot of notes but had no idea, when class was over, what the teacher

   had talked about. Would he give himself a ✓ for #5? _____ What about #6? _____

5. On Friday, there was a test so Dudley did not raise his hand. How should he score #3? _____

   What about #5? _____

Lesson 37 DUDLEY'S GOAL AND PLAN

Overview

In this lesson, students examine several goals and possible ideas for plans for Dudley to participate in his classes. Students are to consider whether the goal is realistic and whether the plan is addressing Dudley's needs. Students should volunteer their own ideas of ways to show that you are participating in class.

Lesson Objectives

- Students will choose an appropriate goal from several possible goals and explain why that goal is most appropriate for the given situation.
- Students will identify appropriate ideas that can be incorporated into a plan and explain why the ideas are most appropriate for the given situation.

Teacher Preparation

Copies of Worksheets 36-2 and 36-3 should already be included in the students' packet of materials.

Lesson Plan

1. Review the previous lesson's assignment by asking students to relate from their own experience problems they have had paying attention in classes and participating actively by various means.

2. Review previous material by asking students to identify Dudley Dreamalot's behavior problem (not participating in class), and state at least one reason why the consequences are not good for Dudley. Ask students to state what they concluded would be a better choice of behaviors for him (to participate actively in his classes).

3. Ask students to locate the packet of Worksheets 36-1 through 36-5 from the previous day and to turn to Worksheet 36-2, "Dudley's Goal."

4. Direct students' attention to the comments at the top. Explain that they will be considering several goals for Dudley and will choose the one that they think is the most appropriate. Discussion questions are

   Goal A
   a. Do you think Dudley can pay attention to everything all day long? (probably not)

b. Does he need to? (no, some information is not necessary to remember forever)

c. How do you feel about this goal for Dudley? (answers will vary)

Goal B

a. Is raising your hand to answer questions a good way to participate? (yes)

b. What would Dudley probably do after he raised his hand once? (think he was done for the day and not pay attention anymore)

c. How do you feel about this goal for Dudley? (answers will vary)

Goal C

a. Is it important to go to class every day to participate? (yes)

b. Is going to class enough of an effort? (no, anyone's body can sit at a desk; it's a passive way to participate)

c. How do you feel about this goal for Dudley? (answers will vary)

Goal D

a. What are some ways that Dudley can actively participate in class? (answers will vary)

b. Are four things enough to show he is participating? (depends on what the ways are)

c. How do you feel about this goal for Dudley? (answers will vary)

4. Direct students' attention to the "Plan" section on Worksheet 36-2, "Dudley's Plan." Call on volunteers to read the comments at the top and the six ideas for plans highlighted on the worksheet. Make sure that students understand that more than one idea can be formulated into a plan. Discussion questions are

Plan A

a. Why is raising your hand to answer a question a good way to show you are actively participating? (it's giving information)

b. Even if the teacher doesn't call on you, how can this help you participate? (your mind will still be answering the question)

c. What do you think of this plan for Dudley? (helpful)

Plan B

a. Why is it important to ask a question in class? (to make sure you understand what's going on)

b. Why is it important to give more information? (to show that you are really listening and understanding what's going on in class)

c. What do you think of this idea? (helpful)

Plan C

a. Is it important to stay awake in class? (yes)

b. Does this show active participation? (staying awake is active, but it isn't really going beyond the minimum!)

c. What do you think of this idea? (minimally helpful)

Plan D

a. Why is looking at the teacher going to help you pay attention? (it will help you keep your mind on the class and what the teacher is saying)

b. Can people look at the teacher and still not be thinking about what he or she is saying? (yes, but your chances are more likely to be paying attention if you are looking at the object of your attention)

c. What do you think of this idea? (helpful)

Plan E

a. How does taking notes show active participation? (it shows a summary of what's important or what happened in the class)

b. Why would writing help someone concentrate on what has been discussed? (as you write, you might repeat what you're writing and thinking)

c. What do you think of this idea? (helpful)

Plan F

a. If Dudley writes notes to Luther, will that help Dudley in his class? (no, there's no connection)

b. Even if Dudley writes notes about the class, will that help Dudley? (probably not—he needs to concentrate on the content of the class, not sending a message to Luther)

c. What do you think of this idea? (not helpful)

5. REVIEW: (a) Ask students to summarize the best goal for Dudley. Ask them to mention some ways that they can show active participation in a class. (b) Ask students to summarize the four most important ideas that could be included in a plan for Dudley (Plans A, B, D, and E) and why they are helpful. (c) Ask students if they see a way that dividing class into before/during/after sections might lend itself to Dudley's plan. Think: What can I do before class to make sure I participate? What can I do during class? What can I do after class? (d) Tell students to file this packet in their folders.

6. ASSIGNMENT: Inform students that they will begin working on a form to help Dudley keep track of his participation in his classes. Ask students to be thinking of ideas they think should be included.

Lesson 38   PARTICIPATING BY USING A CHECKLIST

Overview

Since students have previously been exposed to dividing a task into before/ during/after sections, this knowledge is built upon in Dudley's plan by using a checklist with abbreviated questions directed to the "before" portion of a class, the "during" section (which probably seems the most likely portion to demonstrate participation), and the "after" section.

Students should realize that participating in a class begins before they even enter the classroom by being ready to participate—having their materials with them and being mentally and physically ready to learn. Participation "during" the class can be monitored by tallying the number of times one's hand is raised or, for purposes of streamlining the checklist, merely indicating that this behavior took place. Similarly, creating an awareness of looking at the teacher—even if it only consciously occurs once—increases the likelihood of participating by listening. At the conclusion of the class, participation is extended by examining notes that recorded what went on during class or the content thereof and a brief summary of what was learned or discussed that day. By reducing all these behaviors to a simple checklist task, the student is exposed to six different ways of participating in a class and can monitor himself or herself in each of the areas. With some students, even addressing *one* of these areas would be a major improvement.

For purposes of a student project, you might want to consider targeting one of these ways of participating for some students to concentrate on.

One checklist is presented to students in this lesson. A simple checkmark suffices to indicate whether the behavior occurred that day in that class or not. It is suggested to work with just one class, most likely a class in which there is class discussion, teacher lecture, daily assignments, and fairly straightforward content to summarize.

Lesson Objectives

- Students will identify necessary subtasks for carrying out a specified plan for changing behavior.
- Students will identify an appropriate reward for reaching a goal.
- Students will explain the abbreviated questions on a participation checklist form.
- Students will demonstrate proficiency with recording anecdotal situations correctly on a participation checklist.

Teacher Preparation

Copies of Worksheets 36-4 and 36-5 should already be included in the packet of materials previously distributed to students.

Lesson Plan

1. Review the material previously discussed by asking students the following questions:

   What is Dudley's basic problem? (he daydreams, doesn't participate in class)

   What is Dudley's goal? (to participate by doing at least four things daily in a class)

   What is Dudley's plan? (to raise hand, look at the teacher, take notes, etc.)

2. Inform students that they will be working with a form that will help Dudley organize everything he is supposed to be working on. Ask students to share some ideas as to what information might be necessary to record on a form.

3. To refine Dudley's goal further, the students need to decide how long Dudley should work on actively participating in class and which class should be targeted. Discuss the pros and cons of a class such as math (daily assignments, not a lot of discussion perhaps) and social studies (more discussion, probably still involving daily assignments). For purposes of this set of lessons, Dudley will work on his plan for one week and will target social studies as his class.

4. Ask students to locate the packet of Worksheets 36-1 through 36-5 from their folders and turn to Worksheet 36-4, "Participating in Class."

5. Ask students to think in terms of how they could prepare for class and if that is one way to participate in that class. Alternatively, if they are not prepared materially for class by having their books and pens, how would that affect their ability to participate?

6. Ask students to continue by thinking about how they could participate during the class itself. Some obvious ways have already been discussed and should be reviewed briefly.

7. Finally, ask students how they could show participation in a class at the end of that class. What information was given to them (from the teacher, movies, labs, etc.) and how much of that information can they remember? How will they retain that information?

8. Ask a student volunteer to read the "Keeping Track" section of the work-sheet. Give students a few minutes to complete the task and discuss the items. Answers are Dudley will need to know or do items a, c, e, and g.

9. Direct students' attention to the "Reward" section of the worksheet. Based on the clues given about Dudley, appropriate rewards would focus on softball—time spent playing softball with Luther, perhaps buying a new glove, and so on.

10. Direct students' attention to the "Summary" section of the worksheet. Give students a few minutes to complete the sentences. Answers are

> Dudley has a problem with (participating in class).
>
> He has set a goal of giving himself (checkmarks) during class to show that he is actively participating in the class.
>
> He will work on this goal for (one) week.
>
> To reach his goal, he wants to have (four checkmarks, at least) in his (social studies) class each day.
>
> His plan is to use a (checklist) to make sure he is participating in the class (before), (during), and (after) the class.

11. Direct students' attention to Worksheet 36-5, "Using a Checklist." Ask students to compare this checklist with their own ideas of what should be rated on this type of behavior. Inform students that this is what Dudley will be using to monitor his behavior in his social studies class.

12. Discuss the various elements on the checklist. Make sure students notice the headings for *class* and *week of* at the top.

13. Ask students to expand the abbreviated questions on the checklist. Examples may be

---

1. Materials—Do I have all needed materials for this class?
2. Ready—Am I in my seat with my book open, ready to start?
3. Raise hand—Did I raise my hand to ask/answer a question?
4. Look at teacher—Did I consciously look at the teacher?
5. Notes—Did I take notes on the important information?
6. Summary—Did I write a one-sentence summary of the information discussed today?

---

14. Allow students time to work on the "Try This" section of the worksheet. Answers are

1. No—He does not have all needed materials.
2. No—No matter how often the behavior happens, only one checkmark should be used to show it occurred.
3. Assuming he gave himself checkmarks for the other behaviors, his score would be a 3.
4. Yes—For taking notes; no—he was unable to summarize the notes (time to pinpoint the problem—was he daydreaming or sloppy about notetaking?).
5. He could put "NA" for "not applicable" or an X to show there was not an opportunity to perform that behavior. Same circumstances with 5. If it happens that there is not an opportunity to score four behaviors, that day could either be omitted or scored as a success if he got a checkmark on all of the behaviors that there *was* opportunity to do.

15. REVIEW: (a) Ask students to summarize why it is important to participate in class and the various ways that they discussed of showing active participation. (b) Ask students to summarize briefly Dudley's plan for recording his behavior in social studies. (c) Ask students to demonstrate familiarity with Dudley's checklist by expanding the questions on the checklist. (d) Tell students to file this packet in their folders.

16. ASSIGNMENT: Inform students that on the next day, they will begin taking a look at Dudley in class and deciding whether or not he is participating. As they go throughout their classes until the next meeting, ask students to be aware of ways they are more consciously participating in their classes.

Lesson 39 PRACTICING DUDLEY'S PLAN

Overview

In this lesson, students will observe Dudley's behavior in his social studies class on Monday and Tuesday to see whether or not he is following his plan. Six instances are portrayed that correspond to the six items on the checklist. Students must decide whether the behavior they observe would qualify Dudley giving himself a checkmark on the checklist.

Lesson Objectives

- Students will view examples of a student-model engaging in participating behavior and appropriately mark these behaviors on a checklist.
- Students will state why a specific behavior performed by a student-model is not a participating behavior.

Teacher Preparation

Make enough copies of Worksheet 39-1, "Participating on Monday," and Worksheet 39-2, "Participating on Tuesday," for your students. Students will need a checklist to record Dudley's behavior. If Worksheet 36-5 has not been written on, you may want to have students locate that worksheet in their folder. Worksheet 39-3, "Sample Participation Checklist," is also included for student use on this and the actual student project.

Lesson Plan

1. Review previous material by asking students to list some behaviors that show a student is participating in class. Briefly have students state Dudley's problem, goal, and plan.

2. Distribute Worksheet 39-1 to students. Explain that they will be taking a look at Dudley's behavior on Monday in his social studies class to see how well he is following his plan.

3. Either ask students to locate Worksheet 36-5 for the checklist or distribute Worksheet 39-3. Remind students that Dudley will only give himself one checkmark for each item on the list.

4. Ask for student volunteers to read the comments at the top and each of the boxes on the worksheet. Determine whether or not Dudley would receive a checkmark and give students time to score the checklist appropriately. Answers are

> Box 1—Yes, he apparently has his materials.
>
> Box 2—No, Dudley is not ready to start class; he is talking to Luther.
>
> Box 3—Yes, he is raising his hand to answer a question.
>
> Box 4—No, he is not looking at the teacher.
>
> Box 5—Yes, he is taking important notes.
>
> Box 6—Yes, he mentally summarized what occurred in class.

5. Distribute Worksheet 39-2 to students. Follow the same procedure as for Worksheet 39-1. Answers are

> Box 1—No, he forgot his homework.
>
> Box 2—Yes, he is ready to begin (note pen in hand and paper on desk).
>
> Box 3—Yes, he is raising his hand to make related comments.
>
> Box 4—Yes, he is looking at the teacher.
>
> Box 5—Yes, he is taking notes.
>
> Box 6—No, he does not have the material summarized.

6. Ask if students have any questions about filling out Dudley's checklist. Dudley should have four checkmarks for Monday and four for Tuesday, so he reached his goal for those days.

7. Ask students to discuss any questions or comments about Dudley's participation in class or the participation checklist.

8. REVIEW: (a) Ask students to summarize this lesson's activities by stating what the checklist was used for, how Dudley did, and whether or not he reached his goal. (b) Tell students to file the worksheets in their folders. (c) Inform students that they will have information to complete the checklist for Dudley for the rest of his week.

9. ASSIGNMENT: Ask students to focus consciously on improving one participation behavior in at least one class. You may want to assign *being ready for class by having all materials* as the behavior to focus on. Ask students to jot down what materials are needed for the targeted class and whether or not this was a problem (remembering to bring all needed tools).

PARTICIPATING ON MONDAY

Follow Dudley as he goes through his social studies class on Monday. Is he participating?

PARTICIPATING ON TUESDAY

Watch as Dudley goes to social studies on Tuesday. Is he participating?

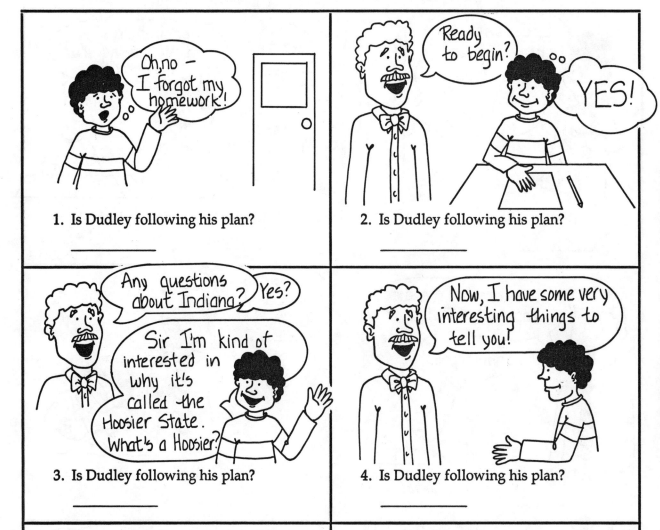

1. Is Dudley following his plan?

_____

2. Is Dudley following his plan?

_____

3. Is Dudley following his plan?

_____

4. Is Dudley following his plan?

_____

5. Is Dudley following his plan?

_____

6. Is Dudley following his plan?

_____

SAMPLE PARTICIPATION CHECKLIST

Class _____   Week of _____

BEFORE CLASS	Mon.	Tues.	Wed.	Thurs.	Fri.
1. Materials?	____	____	____	____	____
2. Ready?	____	____	____	____	____
DURING CLASS					
3. Raise hand?	____	____	____	____	____
4. Look at teacher?	____	____	____	____	____
AFTER CLASS					
5. Notes?	____	____	____	____	____
6. Summary?	____	____	____	____	____
Total (out of 6)	____	____	____	____	____

1. How many checkmarks did I earn on Monday? _____

2. How many checkmarks did I earn on Tuesday? _____

3. How many checkmarks did I earn on Wednesday? _____

4. How many checkmarks did I earn on Thursday? _____

5. How many checkmarks did I earn on Friday? _____

6. Which participation behaviors are not a problem? _____

_____

7. Which participation behaviors are a problem? _____

_____

Lesson 40   HOW DID DUDLEY DO?

Overview

Students will complete the checklist for the remaining three days by being given paragraphs describing Dudley's participating behavior in class. After completing the checklist, evaluation questions are given for the students to consider. Students will find it was fairly easy for Dudley to reach his goal of obtaining only four checkmarks every day, so are then asked to consider Dudley's options at that point. For example, should Dudley concentrate on the participation behaviors that he seemed to have more trouble with (for example, remembering all his materials), or should he strive for six out of six participation behaviors, or should he generalize his behaviors to other classes? Students will, it is hoped, realize that after one has attained a goal, it is a logical next step to expand those skills to other related areas.

Lesson Objectives

- Students will accurately complete a participation checklist and correctly tally the number of successful behaviors.
- Students will evaluate this plan for Dudley by determining whether or not he used the plan and reached his goal.

Teacher Preparation

Make enough copies of Worksheet 40-1, "The Rest of Dudley's Week," and Worksheet 40-2, "Evaluation Form—How Did Dudley Do?," for your students.

Lesson Plan

1. Ask students for their comments about their experiences with having all materials ready for their classes (if this was the targeted behavior from the previous lesson). What materials are generally needed for any class? If the teacher does not specify what to bring, what—in general—would a good student be prepared to bring to class?
2. Inform students that today they will be finishing the rest of Dudley's checklist to see how he is doing with participating in his social studies class this week. They will also be evaluating the plan to see how it would work for them.
3. Ask students to locate Worksheet 39-3, "Sample Participation Checklist," from the previous day (or Worksheet 36-5 if this was the form that

students were using). At this point, the participation behaviors from Monday and Tuesday should be completed on the checklist.

4. Distribute Worksheet 40-1 to students. Ask for student volunteers to read the comments at the top and to supply the missing information from the sentence.

   Dudley's Goal: To get (4) check marks each day in social studies for (one) week.

5. Ask for student volunteers to read the information on the worksheet for each of the three remaining days. As students read the paragraphs, allow time for students to complete their checklists. Discuss any particular questions or comments about the paragraph or completing the checklist. The completed checklist should look like this:

	Mon.	*Tues.*	*Wed.*	*Thurs.*	*Fri.*
1.	✓	—	✓	—	—
2.	—	✓	✓	✓	—
3.	✓	✓	✓	✓	✓
4.	—	✓	✓	✓	✓
5.	✓	✓	X	✓	✓
6.	✓	—	✓	—	✓
Totals:	4	4	5	4	4

6. Distribute Worksheet 40-2 to students. Ask for volunteers to read and answer the evaluation questions. Suggested answers are

1. Yes (4 out of 6).

2. Yes.

3. Yes (his goal was at least four behaviors each day).

4. Possible—although it involved six different behaviors so he always had something to work on improving; on only one behavior (two, if you discount the day of the test) was there a perfect score throughout the week.

5. 1—having all his materials for class; there were three instances in which he did not have everything he needed.

6. 3—raising his hand (there were no days on which he failed to do this); 5—taking notes (he only missed once and that was the day of the test so there was no opportunity).

7. Opinion (it wouldn't hurt him to continue for another week to try to stabilize some of the behaviors).

8. Goal: Dudley will bring all needed materials to class four out of five times in one week.

9. Goal: Dudley will score five out of six on participation behaviors each day in social studies for one week.

10. Goal: Dudley will score at least four participation behaviors in his science class each day for one week.

11. Opinion.

7. REVIEW: (a) Have students offer their opinions as to Dudley's plan, goal, and behavior change. Ask for their ideas for using a similar plan in their classes. What would be helpful? What would not work for them? (b) Explain to students that in the next lesson, they will begin working on monitoring their own participation in classes much like Dudley did. They should be thinking about what behaviors they will need to improve and how they could go about starting to do that. (c) Tell students to file their worksheets in their folders.

8. ASSIGNMENT: Ask students to make a list of the participation behaviors they think are most important for their classes and to put a star by the ones they feel they need the most help with.

THE REST OF DUDLEY'S WEEK

Fill out the rest of Dudley's checklist after reading about how he participated in social studies during the rest of the week.

DUDLEY'S GOAL: To get —————— check marks each day in

social studies for —————— week(s).

Wednesday

Dudley knew there would be a test that day, so he brought his pencil and some paper to class. He knew he didn't need his book that day. He went to his seat, got the paper out, and noticed that his pencil wasn't very sharp. He sharpened it and was back in his seat before the bell rang. The teacher asked if there were any questions. Dudley raised his hand to ask a question about the largest city in Wisconsin. He looked carefully at the teacher as he gave the answer. There were no notes to take, but Dudley worked hard on the test. When he was finished, he summed up the day by thinking about the things that were asked on the test.

Thursday

Dudley brought his book to class, but forgot to bring his paper, so he had to borrow some from Luther. He was in his seat when the bell rang with paper and pencil ready to go. The teacher began talking about how the class did on the test. Dudley watched very carefully as the teacher walked back and forth in front of the room. Dudley began looking out of the window when he saw some kids going out to P.E., and he realized he wasn't listening anymore. He raised his hand to ask the teacher to repeat what he had just said, which the teacher gladly did. Dudley began to write down what the teacher said so he would remember. After the bell rang, Dudley closed his book and went to his next class.

Friday

Dudley was late to class because he was talking in the hall to Holly. He also realized he had forgotten a pencil. Once in class, however, he raised his hand twice to ask questions and concentrated very hard on watching the teacher point out cities on the U.S. map. He wrote down the names of the cities that were written on the board. At the end of class, Dudley reviewed the cities that were talked about and knew they were the largest cities in their states.

EVALUATION FORM—HOW DID DUDLEY DO?

Use Dudley's checklist to answer the following questions about
how well Dudley's plan worked for him.

1. Did Dudley reach his intended score on Monday? _____

2. Did Dudley reach his intended score on the rest of the days of this week? _____

3. Did Dudley reach his goal for this week? _____

4. Do you think this goal was too easy for Dudley? _____

   _____

5. What participation behavior did Dudley seem to have the most trouble doing? _____

   _____

6. Which two behaviors seemed to be the easiest for Dudley to do? _____

   _____

7. Do you think Dudley should continue this plan for another week or try something else?

   _____

8. What would be a good goal for Dudley if he wanted to concentrate on improving the one

   behavior that he had the most trouble with? _____

   _____

9. What would be a good goal for Dudley if he wanted to concentrate on being the best social

   studies participant that he could be? _____

   _____

   _____

10. What would be a good goal for Dudley if he wanted to try out these skills in another class?

    _____

    _____

11. What would you use or change about this plan to use for yourself? _____

    _____

    _____

Lesson 41 APPLICATION—GET INVOLVED!

Overview

By this lesson, students should be anticipating what is coming! Dudley Dreamalot successfully improved his behavior by participating more actively before class, during class, and at the end of class. The checklist that Dudley used to monitor his behavior was probably a bit more complex than your students will use for their projects. If students can pinpoint one main participation behavior they would like to work on, that would be a sufficient start. It would be helpful, however, for students to select one of the six behaviors that was outlined on Dudley's checklist. Your considerations should include

1. Do you want all students to work on monitoring the same behavior? Whether students specifically need to improve that behavior may be a secondary consideration if students need the practice in monitoring behavior.

2. How do you want students to record their behavior? Some behaviors, such as raising one's hand or looking at the teacher, can simply be tallied. Others, such as having materials and summarizing the notes, can be recorded on a yes/no chart.

3. If students select only one participation behavior to work on, it is important to have them practice that behavior as many times throughout the day as possible. Thus, that one behavior may be monitored for several classes for additional practice.

4. Students may not be completely accurate on their self-monitoring skills. Although honest and sincere in their attempts, some students just need a lot of practice in self-evaluation. One way to ease the student through this without completely discouraging him is to have partners check on each other. Whereas one student may walk in the door of the class claiming to be ready to start, another may not be ready until his pencil is sharpened, his book is open, and he has ended his conversation with the boy next to him. It is most important to define your terms: What is meant (in your class, if nowhere else) by "being ready" to start class? What will you accept as "notes" or a "summary of the day"? By conveying your expectations clearly to students, you will greatly ease their task of living up to what you want and knowing whether or not they have evaluated themselves accurately. It takes time!

Students should carry out their projects for at least two weeks, periodically sharing their problems and successes in class. From time to time, if possible, a surprise "teacher agreement check" can be conducted to see if the students' checklists match those of the teacher. If students have a different teacher for a class in

203

which they are trying to participate, it may be helpful to alert that teacher to look for (and comment upon) improved effort in that area.

Lesson Objectives

- Students will devise a plan for improving their participation in a class or classes.

- Students will set and reach a realistic goal for their participation project.

- Students will accurately self-monitor this selected behavior with 90% accuracy.

Teacher Preparation

1. Make enough copies of Worksheet 41-1, "Student Worksheet" (two pages), for your students.

2. You may want to run off additional copies of Worksheet 39-3, "Sample Participation Checklist," for students to refer to as they begin thinking about their own projects.

3. You might want to copy the following symbols on the chalkboard to refer to as the different sections of the worksheet are discussed.

Lesson Plan

1. Inform students that they are now going to begin work on a project that will help them participate more in their classes. Explain that they will be formulating a goal and plan much like Dudley's.

2. Distribute Worksheet 41-1 to students.

3. Discuss the questions on the worksheet and allow students time to record their opinions and/or commitments to making a plan and goal.

   a. Question 2: Students are asked to think about each of the six behaviors that was part of Dudley's checklist.

b. Question 3: Have students select the one behavior that is of most concern to them. You may want to monitor this closely to make sure that, in your opinion, the student has selected the most appropriate behavior for himself or herself.

c. Question 4: Several consequences have previously been discussed. While some students may feel that they are not harming anyone by silently sitting at a desk, remind them that participation should be an active behavior.

d. Question 6: Students should specify how they will choose to participate in class by mentioning one of the six behaviors on the checklist.

e. Question 7: Remind students to write a goal that involves a specific number of times that a behavior will happen or a percentage of the time that this behavior will happen.

f. Question 8: Have students select a goal they can probably attain within two weeks.

g. Question 9: Students should mention that they will change their behavior by participating more (in the specific way they have selected as their target behavior).

h. Question 10: Students should specify plan ideas that involve positive steps toward achieving their goal, for example, getting to class early, having all books within easy reach, counting the number of times they raise their hand in class, and so on.

i. Question 13: Students should make a checklist or other recording form suitable for the target behavior. If some portions of Dudley's form are applicable, students can revise Worksheet 39-3, "Sample Participation Checklist."

j. Question 14: Students should summarize their goal. An example might read: At the end of *two weeks,* I will look at my *tally card* and see whether or not I am *raising my hand three times a day in my science class.* If my score is *success eight out of ten days,* I have reached my goal.

k. Question 15: In addition to a personal reward, you may want to offer a class reward for students to work for.

4. Allow time for any specific questions, comments, or problems with the worksheet or development of plans, goals, or forms.

5. Tell students to file their worksheets in their folders.

6. Select a starting date for the students to begin carrying out their projects. Check to make sure that each student is starting with appropriate goals and a recording sheet that is simple but meaningful.

7. Class time should be set aside daily to discuss the projects and specific problems that may arise from time to time. Ask students periodically if

they find that actively participating in their classes has helped them. In what way? Keep the following points in mind:

a. Self-recording is work! Students may initially find the assignment (and the power) fun, but they need to view it also as a task for which they are accountable. They need to be as accurate as possible.

b. As problems with self-recording arise, it may be helpful to have students role-play the questionable situation and decide as a class whether or not the student met the criteria for "participating."

c. When teacher and student evaluations of participating in a class concur, praise the student—not for agreeing with you but for accurate recording. The idea is not to "think like the teacher," but to view oneself and one's behavior objectively.

STUDENT WORKSHEET

1. *Behavior:* Is this behavior, active participation in class, something that would help make you a better student?

   (B) _____

2. Do you have difficulty with the following behaviors:

   a. Remembering materials for your classes? _____

   b. Being ready when class starts? _____

   c. Raising your hand to ask or answer questions? _____

   d. Keeping your attention on the teacher? _____

   e. Taking notes in class? _____

   f. Summarizing what the class was about? _____

3. If you chose only *one* of the above behaviors as your biggest problem, which would it be?

   _____

4. *Consequences:* What are the consequences when you are in class in body, but do nothing to participate in class? _____

   (B) _____

5. *Choices:* Can you *choose* to participate? _____

6. How? _____

7. *Goal:* What goal will you set for yourself?

   ☆ My goal is to: _____

8. How long do you think it will take you to reach your goal? _____

9. How are you going to change your behavior to reach your goal? _____

   _____

10. *Plan:* What are some ideas for your plan to reach your goal?

    I could _____

    I could _____

    I could _____

11. Choose a plan. I pick _____

12. What do you need to do or get to carry out your plan? _____

    _____

    _____

    _____

13. *Keeping Track:* How will you *keep track* of your behavior and plan? (You can use a ckecklist like

    Dudley's or make up your own.) _____

    _____

    _____

    _____

14. How will you know when you have reached your goal?

    At the end of _____, I will look at my _____
                     (how long?)   (checklist, chart?)

    and see whether or not I am _____.
                                         (participating—how?)

    If my score is _____, I have reached my goal.
                      (number or %)

15. *Reward:* How will you reward yourself? _____

    When will you reward yourself? _____

    This plan and goal will be evaluated on _____.
                                                        (date)

Lesson 42   EVALUATION OF YOUR PROJECT

Overview

After the students have conducted their projects for about two weeks, the class should share their findings and experiences with each other. Anecdotes are often a good way to convey the success of participating in class rather than merely looking at a checklist or graph. Students should be encouraged to respond subjectively. It is hoped that students who were inactive participants have, in some small way, improved to the point that they now realize they are important to the class and can indeed offer a contribution.

Lesson Objectives

- Students will determine whether or not they have reached their goal.
- Students will specify modifications for their plan to improve it if they would be continuing it.

Teacher Preparation

Make enough copies of Worksheet 28-1, "Evaluation Questions," for your students.

Lesson Plan

1. Have students assemble all paperwork that was used in their projects (for example, recording forms, notebooks, summary sheets, etc.).
2. Distribute Worksheet 28-1 to students.
3. Inform students that the class will now be sharing their experiences with being better participants in their classes. Ask for a general class consensus of whether or not the projects were helpful.
4. Discuss the questions on the worksheet. Volunteers may elaborate on their experiences with their plans. All students should complete the evaluation form.
5. Conclude the discussion by asking students what behavior(s) they think they would choose to work on next if they continued with this project. What parts of the plan would they keep the same? What would have to be different?
6. Tell students to file their worksheets and other paperwork in their folders.

7. You may want to give each student a grade on the project based on their paperwork and change in behavior.

8. ASSIGNMENT: Inform students that the final lesson will ask them to complete a student survey where they will rate themselves according to how good a student they think they are now. In the time between now and the next lesson, they should be thinking about how they have improved as students and why.

Lesson 43   ARE YOU A BETTER STUDENT?

Overview

In this final lesson, students are given the opportunity to reflect on the assignments, projects, and techniques they have worked on to determine whether or not they have become better students. Students are asked to compare their subjective feelings about their student skills at the beginning of the course by referring to Worksheet 3-2, "Student Behavior Survey," which they completed before really learning about how to be a better student, with their feelings about their skills now at the end of the course, after they have had a lot of opportunities to learn and apply their skills.

Students ideally should not only have learned a few basic skills for improving their behavior at school, but also have acquired a sense of competence in their problem-solving abilities, so that when new problems arise that they want to resolve, they can rely on a problem-solving technique to make a goal, devise a plan, and systematically carry out a self-management program.

This course of study is only the beginning of a long road toward making reluctant students "better" students. A lot of effort is required, not only on the part of the students, but on the part of the teacher. Initially, most of the energy for striving toward behavior change needs to come from the teacher. After students have experienced success and the feeling of competence and power that are derived from managing one's own behavior, students will then have a reserve of energy that can supplement the teacher's. After all, the work you have put into showing students how they can become better students will convince you that you are a better teacher!

Lesson Objectives

- Students will complete a student behavior survey based on their experiences with this course.
- Students will identify areas of strengths and weaknesses in their school skills.
- Students will identify basic components of behavior change programs that they would involve in their next attempt to improve their student skills.

Teacher Preparation

1. Make enough copies of Worksheet 43-1, "Student Behavior Survey," for your students.
2. Familiarize yourself with Worksheet 3-2, "Student Behavior Survey," that your students will use to compare their ratings of their behaviors.

Lesson Plan

1. Inform students that in this final lesson, they are going to evaluate themselves as to whether they think they are now better students or not.

2. Distribute Worksheet 43-1 to students. Allow students time to complete the items on the survey.

3. Ask students to locate Worksheet 3-2 in their folders. Explain that they may find their answers are different in some areas. Allow time for students to review this worksheet.

4. Discuss the following questions:

   a. What things did you list as areas that you are good in at school on the first worksheet?

   b. Were the same things listed for Question 3 on the second worksheet?

   c. What things did you learn to do better?

   d. Why are those behaviors easier now?

   e. What things did you list as being hard for you at school?

   f. Are those things still problems for you (see Question 4 on the second survey)?

   g. If so, why? If not, why not? Did the projects help?

   h. What was the main thing you wanted to improve about yourself at school before this course?

   i. What is the main thing now that you would like to improve about yourself at school?

   j. If you wanted to change another behavior at school to be an even better student, what are some things you would do?

5. Allow time for final comments or discussion questions from students.

6. Praise students for their fine work on the assignments and their individual projects. Remind them to keep using their skills!

7. Tell students to file both surveys in their folders.

8. If desired, you may want to collect the folders and provide a grade for neatly kept folders with all worksheets in chronological order.

STUDENT BEHAVIOR SURVEY

Please fill out this survey honestly. When you are finished, compare your answers with those from Worksheet 3–2, the first survey you filled out at the beginning of the course.

1. Do you think you are a better student now than before you worked on these lessons? ————

2. Why or why not? ——————————————————————————

———————————————————————————————————

———————————————————————————————————

3. What are some things you have learned to do better?

   a. ——————————————————————————————————

   b. ——————————————————————————————————

   c. ——————————————————————————————————

4. What are still some problems for you that stop you from being a better student?

   a. ——————————————————————————————————

   b. ——————————————————————————————————

   c. ——————————————————————————————————

5. What is one main thing now that you would like to improve about yourself at school?

———————————————————————————————————

———————————————————————————————————

———————————————————————————————————

6. How would you go about improving that behavior?

———————————————————————————————————

———————————————————————————————————

———————————————————————————————————

Appendix

SKILLS INDEX
AND ADDITIONAL FORMS

Luther Lateagain's Problem: Turning in Assignments on Time

RELATED PROBLEMS	SKILL TO BE LEARNED	FORM
Can't keep track of daily assignments in class	Keeping an assignment sheet	"Sample Assignment Chart" (Worksheet 27-2)
Forgets homework assignments	Keeping a homework sheet	"Homework Sheet"
Has no knowledge of how his performance is in class gradewise	Keeping a running record of grades/points	"Recordkeeping Form"
Loses daily assignments or doesn't have materials for class	Maintaining daily checklist of materials and locations	"Materials Checklist"

Holly Hoocares' Problem: Doing Careful Work

RELATED PROBLEMS	SKILL TO BE LEARNED	FORM
Doesn't follow directions throughout assignment	Cueing self to continue to follow directions	"Sample Daily Grade Card and Question Card" (Worksheet 33-4)
Doesn't know her daily assignment grades	Keeping track of daily grades	"Sample Daily Grade Card and Question Card" (Worksheet 33-4)
Does careless work in math assignments	Proofreading math assignments for key elements	"Proofreading for Math"
Does careless work on written assignments	Proofreading written assignments for key elements (mechanics)	"Proofreading Written Work (Mechanics)"
Doesn't provide appropriate answers for questions on assignments	Proofreading written work for key elements (content)	"Proofreading Written Work (Content)"

Dudley Dreamalot's Problem: Participating in Class

RELATED PROBLEMS	SKILL TO BE LEARNED	FORM
Has poor overall class participation, preparation, and retention	Overall monitoring of participation skills	"Participation Checklist" (Worksheet 39-3)
Doesn't raise his hand to indicate readiness to participate	Counting number of times hand is raised to indicate readiness to participate	"Tally Sheet"
Doesn't pay attention to task	Self-monitoring attention to task	"Yes/No Chart"
Doesn't retain class information	Summarizing class facts or details	"Topic Summary Sheet"
Needs objective feedback on his overall behavior in class	Recording behavior (by student, teacher, or both)	"How Was I in Class Today?"

Name —————————————— **Week of** ——————————————

HOMEWORK SHEET

MONDAY	
Class/Subject	*Assignment*
————————————	————————————
Parent signature	Student signature

TUESDAY	
Class/Subject	*Assignment*
————————————	————————————
Parent signature	Student signature

WEDNESDAY	
Class/Subject	*Assignment*
————————————	————————————
Parent signature	Student signature

THURSDAY	
Class/Subject	*Assignment*
————————————	————————————
Parent signature	Student signature

FRIDAY	
Class/Subject	*Assignment*
————————————	————————————
Parent signature	Student signature

Name _____ Class/Subject _____

RECORDKEEPING FORM

DATE	ASSIGNMENT	POSSIBLE POINTS	MY POINTS	% OR GRADE

Name _____ Date _____

MATERIALS CHECKLIST

Class/Subject _____

These are the materials I will need for this class on _____ :
(day/date)

1. _____

2. _____

3. _____

4. _____

5. _____

This is where I will put and find the materials before class:

1. _____

2. _____

3. _____

4. _____

5. _____

Before class on _____, I have these materials:
(day/date)

1. _____

2. _____

3. _____

4. _____

5. _____

I   am   am not   prepared for class today.

PROOFREADING FOR MATH

What will your math teacher be looking for when he or she grades your assignment? Put an X next to each item that your teacher will think is important. Then check your assignment over and see how it compares.

Assignment: _____

IMPORTANT ITEMS   MY EVALUATION OF THIS ASSIGNMENT

____ 1. name on paper   _____

____ 2. date   _____

____ 3. class or subject   _____

____ 4. page number   _____

____ 5. used pen   _____

____ 6. used pencil   _____

____ 7. used correct paper   _____

____ 8. paper looks neat   _____

____ 9. copied the problem   _____

____ 10. showed my work   _____

____ 11. circled the answer   _____

____ 12. left space between problems   _____

____ 13. didn't skip any problems   _____

____ 14. marked unsure answers   _____

____ 15. spot-checked some problems   _____

____ 16. _____   _____

____ 17. _____   _____

____ 18. _____   _____

PROOFREADING WRITTEN WORK (MECHANICS)

What will your teacher be looking for when he or she grades your written work? Put an X next to each item that your teacher will think is important. Then check your assignment over and see how it compares.

Assignment: _____

IMPORTANT ITEMS	MY EVALUATION OF THIS ASSIGNMENT
____ 1. name on paper	_____
____ 2. date	_____
____ 3. class or subject	_____
____ 4. page number	_____
____ 5. used pen	_____
____ 6. used pencil	_____
____ 7. used correct paper	_____
____ 8. used cursive handwriting	_____
____ 9. paper looks neat	_____
____ 10. careful handwriting	_____
____ 11. proper capitalization	_____
____ 12. used correct punctuation	_____
____ 13. new paragraphs indented	_____
____ 14. spelled words correctly	_____
____ 15. used words correctly (words "sound" right when read out loud)	_____
____ 16. has a title	_____
____ 17. has left and right margins	_____
____ 18. _____	_____

_____

PROOFREADING WRITTEN WORK (CONTENT)

What will your teacher be looking for when he or she grades your answers to questions? Put an X next to each item that your teacher will think is important. Then check your assignment over and see how it compares.

Assignment: _____

IMPORTANT ITEMS   MY EVALUATION OF THIS ASSIGNMENT

____ 1. name on paper   _____

____ 2. date   _____

____ 3. page number   _____

____ 4. used pen   _____

____ 5. used pencil   _____

____ 6. copied the question   _____

____ 7. answer in complete sentences _____

____ 8. gave the entire answer   _____
        (not just one item if
        question asked for more)

____ 9. answered every question   _____

____ 10. understood what the   _____
        question was looking for
        (fact versus opinion, dates,
        names, places, lists, and so on)

____ 11. answers make sense (it   _____
        "sounds" like an answer
        when read out loud)

____ 12. used appropriate source to _____
        answer question (text,
        workbook, dictionary, map
        versus guessing)

____ 13. _____   _____

        _____

____ 14. _____   _____

        _____

Name _____ Date _____

TALLY SHEET

Class: _____

Circle the behavior monitored:

How many times did I—

    a. raise my hand to ask a question? _____

    b. raise my hand to answer a question? _____

    c. raise my hand to make an appropriate comment? _____

YES/NO CHART

Question: _____
        (Am I paying attention?)   (Am I doing my work?)

TIME INTERVAL

1. _____ Yes   No

2. _____ Yes   No

3. _____ Yes   No

4. _____ Yes   No

5. _____ Yes   No

6. _____ Yes   No

7. _____ Yes   No

8. _____ Yes   No

9. _____ Yes   No

10. _____ Yes   No

Name _____ Week of _____

TOPIC SUMMARY SHEET

Class/Subject: _____

MONDAY	Topic(s): _____
Important Facts or Details	*Book Pages*

TUESDAY	Topic(s): _____
Important Facts or Details	*Book Pages*

WEDNESDAY	Topic(s): _____
Important Facts or Details	*Book Pages*

THURSDAY	Topic(s): _____
Important Facts or Details	*Book Pages*

FRIDAY	Topic(s): _____
Important Facts or Details	*Books Pages*

Name _____ Date _____

HOW WAS I IN CLASS TODAY?

Behavior Score: + or 0

Class Periods

	1	2	3	4	5	6	7
1. Entered room appropriately							
2. Had proper materials							
3. In seat when bell rang							
4. Used quiet voice							
5. Used materials quietly							
6. Followed directions							
7. Respected teacher							
8. Got along with peers							
9. Used time wisely							
10. Completed assignment							

Total points for class: _____ _____ _____ _____ _____ _____

Total points for the day: _____

_____
Parent signature